Allan Webber is the Financial Markets Courses Director in the professional training arm of City University Business School, London. He is responsible for public and in-house securities markets related courses and teaches in this area. He has written texts for bond and fixed interest markets, futures and options, investment analysis and fund management. He has also advised the Securities and Futures Authority on syllabus content for their registered persons qualifications. His PhD covered aspects of government policy and he has written extensively about monetary economics and banking.

DICTIONARY OF FUTURES & OPTIONS

Alan Webber

Vision Books
(Incorporating Orient Paperbacks)
New Delhi • Bombay • Hyderabad

[Authorised edition for sale in India, Pakistan, Bangladesh, Nepal and Sri Lanka only.]

ISBN 81-7094-331-0

© Alan Webber

ALL RIGHTS RESERVED. No part of this publication may be reproduced, stored in a retrieval system, or transmitted, in any form or by any means, electronic, mechanical, photocopying, recording or otherwise, without the prior written permission of the publisher and the copyright holder.

This edition published in arrangement with
Probus Publishing Company, U.S.A. by
Vision Books Pvt. Ltd.
(Incorporating Orient Paperbacks)
24 Feroze Gandhi Road, Lajpat Nagar III,
New Delhi-110024 (India)
Phone: (+91-11) 6836470/80
Fax: (+91-11) 6836490
E-mail: visionbk@del2.vsnl.net.in

Printed at
Rashtra Rachna Printers
C-88, Ganesh Nagar, Pandav Nagar Complex,
Delhi-110092 (India).

Contents

Foreword — vii

A-Z of terms — 1

Appendix 1 — 193
Option premium value components (call option)

Appendix 2 — 194
Option strategy profit and loss diagrams

Appendix 3 — 198
Option pricing model output

Appendix 4 — 200
Profile of a call option vs. underlying price

Appendix 5 — 203
Position characteristics

Appendix 6 — 204
Characteristics of volatility spreads

Appendix 7 — 205
Evaluating a position

Foreword

This publication is presented as a dictionary, and hopefully fulfils that role by providing concise explanations of many terms. However, in some cases—notably, option strategies—there is clearly a need for more detail. As a result, these entries have been expanded in order that the nature and impact of such strategies can be discussed in depth. Furthermore, the appendices contain graphics which will hopefully enable interested readers to absorb the intricacies of option scenarios in a quick, but reasonably thorough, manner.

The world's major futures and options exchanges are listed in this dictionary. For a full and complete reference to exchange contracts and structures, see *The World's Futures & Options Markets*, Nick Battley (Ed.), Probus Europe, 1994.

Caution

Whilst the greatest care has been taken in compiling this glossary, various terms have more than one meaning, usually across different markets, and new usages and definitions also develop.

Thus, before any investment decisions are made advice should be sought from a professional. The authors and publishers accept no responsibility for errors or omissions in this publication, nor for its use in trading, investment, or any other purpose whatsoever.

A

A$
Textual abbreviation for Australian dollar(s).

AA
Against actuals. *See* **exchange for physicals**.

AAPP
Average All Pig Price. (UK)

abandon
The act of the option holder in electing not to exercise an option.

ABI
Association of Italian Bankers.

absolute rate
A bid/offer made on euronotes which is not expressed in relation to a particular funding base such as Libor or US domestic certificate of deposit rates, i.e., '9.125%' instead of 'Libor + 0.005%'.

acceptance
Agreement of intention to carry out a transaction.

Account
The London Stock Exchange Account Period. The London Stock Exchange divides the year into two-week dealing periods. Any equity deals made in an Account are settled on the second Monday of the following two-week Account. It is planned to be replaced by 10-day rolling settlement in 1994, and later by 5-day rolling settlement.

Account day
The day in an Account period in which all bargains from the previous Account are settled. The second Monday of the Account period. (LSE)

account executive
General term for a broker or agent who services specific clients.

account sale
A statement by a broker to a commodity customer when a futures transaction is closed out. Sometimes referred to as a *P&S (purchase and sale statement)*, it shows the net profit or loss on the transaction, with commission and other proper charges set forth and taken into account.

accrued interest
That part of the next coupon payment on a bond which accrues to a bondholder during the period held. For example, if a bond is held it for four months of a semi-annual coupon period, the holder will be entitled to 4/12th of the quoted annual coupon. The holder will be fully compensated for this when the bond is sold. Conventions for calculating accrued interest vary from market to market. For gilts, it is the number of days accrued as a proportion of a year of 365 days, multiplied by the coupon per £100 nominal value (actual/365). For eurobonds, each month is considered to have 30 days, with each year consisting of twelve such months (30/360).

accumulate
Traders are said to accumulate contracts when they add to their original market positions.

acreage allotment
Government limitations on the planted acreage of some basic crops.

actuals
Physical commodities, also commodities readily available. The commodity itself as opposed to a futures contract.

additional margin
Intra-day margin call facility used by a clearing house in conditions of exceptional volatility.

adjusted futures price
The cash price equivalent reflected in the current futures price. This is calculated by taking the futures prices times the conversion factor for the particular financial instrument (e.g., bond or note) being delivered.

AE
See **account executive**.

AFFM
See **Australian Financial Futures Market**.

afloat
Physical commodity in harbour or in transit in a vessel. Commodities on board, ready to sail.

AFOFs
Authorized futures and options funds. (UK)

against actuals (AA)
See **exchange for physicals.**

aggregate exercise price
The exercise price of an option contract multiplied by the number of units of underlying covered by the option contract.

aggressor brokerage (currency asset markets)
Where brokerage is charged to the party which acts on the broker's market (i.e. hits the bid or takes the offer).

Agrarische Termijnmarkt Amsterdam (ATA)
A Dutch exchange which lists futures contracts on live hogs, piglets and potatoes.

AIBD
Association of International Bond Dealers, now called the **International Securities Market Association.**

alligator spread
Any spread in the options markets that 'eats the investor alive' because of its high commission costs. The term may be used when a broker advocates or arranges a combination of calls and puts that generate so much commission that the client is unlikely or unable to obtain a profit net of commission even if the markets move as anticipated.

allocated bullion holding accounts
With allocated holding accounts, specific bars are physically segregated and set aside with detailed weight lists and assays. The costs of maintaining such accounts are at the discretion of the listed institution. *See* **unallocated bullion holding accounts.**

allocation
The process of assigning an executed trade back to its originating principal.

allocation chain
The chain of parties interested in a specific transaction from its originator, intermediary parties where applicable and the executing broker.

allocation claim
A claim from an interested party in an allocation chain to title of an executed trade.

allocation give up
Assignment from an intermediary to a transaction claimant or originator.

all or none (AON)
An order that must be filled in full or not at all.

all-or-nothing options
Digital options that pay out a set amount if the underlying asset is above or below the strike price at expiry. (The amount the option is in-the-money is irrelevant since it is a fixed amount that is paid out). *See also* **digital options**.

allowances
The discounts (premiums) allowed for grades or locations of a commodity lower (higher) than the par or a basis grade or location specified in the futures contract.

American option
An option that can be exercised at any time prior to expiry.

American Stock Exchange (AMEX)
Located in New York, AMEX lists equity, equity index, (and sector indices) options. It should not be confused with the New York Stock Exchange (NYSE), which is an entirely separate entity.

AMEX
See **American Stock Exchange**.

amortize
A method of allocating over the life of an open contract, income received or given up at maturity.

amortizing cap
See **amortizing option**.

amortizing collar
See **amortizing option**.

amortizing option
An interest rate or swap option whose notional amount (underlying value) decreases during the life of the option. This includes amortizing caps, collars and swaptions.

AOM
See **Australian Options Market**.

AON
See **all or none order**.

approved delivery
Any bank, stockyard, mill, store, warehouse, plant, elevator or other depository that is authorized by an exchange for the delivery of commodities tendered on futures contracts.

APT
LIFFE's Automated Pit Trading System, it operates from terminals in members' offices from 4.30 to 6.00pm after the floor has closed. Its displays replicate floor trading.

arbitrage
The purchase (or sale) of security or contract in one market and the simultaneous sale (or purchase) of a synthetic version or the same amount in another to take advantage of price differentials.

arbitrageur
One who practices the trading technique of arbitrage.

arbitration
The procedure for settling disputes between members, or between members and customers.

ARS
Standard foreign exchange code for Argentine peso(s).

ascending triangle
A chart pattern that signals a continuation of an uptrend.

Asian option
See **average rate option**.

ask
An indication of willingness, made at a given moment, to sell a futures or options contract, or other asset, at a specific price. (Also known as *offer*).

ask price
Price at which a seller will trade, also called *offer price*. The price at which someone is prepared to sell, or is making a price offering to sell. Some exchange displays mark such offered prices with an (A).

assay
Analysis of metals submitted in order to arrive at confirmation of their purity. May be done by any of several methods (spectroscopy, etc.) and produces a list of other elements found in the sample, and their percentage of the whole.

assign
To make options sellers perform their obligations in assuming short futures positions or selling the underlying cash market (as sellers of call options) or long futures positions or buying the underlying cash market (as sellers of a put option).

assignment notice
Formal notification from the exchange clearing house to writers requiring fulfilment of their contractual obligation to buy or sell the underlying asset.

associated person (AP)
An individual who solicits orders, customers, or customer funds (or who supervises persons performing such duties) on behalf of a futures commission merchant, an introducing broker, a commodity trading adviser, or a commodity pool operator in the US.

associate member
See **associate trade member**.

associate trade member
A category of exchange membership that does not confer trading or voting rights. This membership category is for the underlying industry, e.g. oil on IPE or metals on LME. It is likely to be significantly represented on the board of the exchange.

ASTM
The American Society for Testing Materials. The official body in the USA for laying down standards as to purity as well as methods to be adopted for sampling and assaying.

ASX
Australian Stock Exchange.

at
The key preposition in a trader's quotation signifying an order for sale, e.g. "thirty [lots/contracts of] Sep[tember] *at* ten [price]". *See also* **for**.

ATA
See **Agrarische Termijnmarkt Amsterdam**.

at a premium (foreign exchange and currency deposit markets)
A currency which is more expensive to purchase forward than for spot delivery.

Atlantic option
The name given by Westminster Equity to an option where the exercise style, American or European can vary over the life of the option depending on the value of the underlying.

ATS
Standard foreign exchange code for Austrian schilling(s).

at the market
See **market order**.

at-the-money
An option with an exercise price equal or near to the current underlying futures, financial asset, or commodity price.

ATX
Austrian Traded Index, traded as an option on ÖTOB.

AUD
Standard foreign exchange code for Australian dollar(s).

Australian Financial Futures Market (AFFM)
Located in Sydney, the AFFM is part of the Australian Stock Exchange. It lists equity index futures and options.

Australian Options Market (AOM)
Located in Sydney, the AOM is part of the Australian Stock Exchange. It lists equity options and index options.

authorized floor member (London Commodity Exchange)
A member of the market who may, subject to the rules, be licensed to trade on the market floor or in the automated trading system of any division of the market (but does not include a local floor member or a market-maker member).

automatic exercise
Many exchanges will automatically exercise in-the-money options without requiring notice. Contracts at-the-money or the first in-the-money series are not subject to automatic exercise because the holder may find this unprofitable once transactions costs and commissions are taken into account. In London the holder may notify at which price automatic exercise can take place.

average cap (average rate cap)
A cap on an average interest rate over a given period as distinct from the rate existing at the end of the period. *See also* **average rate option**.

average rate option (Asian option)
An option that gives the holder the right to deal at the average price of the underlying asset over the life of the option. Four variables have to be agreed between the buyer and seller, being the premium, strike price, exchange rate or commodity price or interest rate etc., and the sampling interval. At the expiry of the option, the average spot rate is calculated and compared with the strike price. If in-the-money, a cash payment is then made to the buyer representing the difference between the two rates times the face value of the option. The volatility of an average rate is clearly lower than the actual price of the underlying. As such, these options are cheaper than standard options. An average rate option would be used to hedge regular cashflows, say a company's monthly foreign exchange income, or borrowing cost, to achieve a budgeted average rate for the year. These are normally European-style exercise.

B

back-pricing
Regular customers of a metal smelter or refiner or other supplier may be permitted to price a proportion of their month's intake on the known LME settlement price quoted the day previous to the date of pricing the intake. The proportion to be so priced is laid down in the contract, and the consumers—if they wishes to avail themselves of the facility—must place their order before commencement of official trading on the LME on the date in question.

backspreads
Calls and puts can be combined on a ratioed basis whereby the number of calls (or puts) purchased exceeds the number of calls (or puts) written. This is achieved by reversing the call ratio spread (or put ratio spread) thereby creating backspreads. *See* **call ratio backspread** and **put ratio backspread**.

backwardation
When the spot or nearby prices are higher than those for future delivery months. Usually caused by delays in shipment thus creating shortages in available supplies. Opposite of *contango*. There is a theory that when the market is in equilibrium as to supply and demand, a backwardation is a logical state of affairs since producers selling forward in order to hedge their own anticipated supplies to the market will expect to pay a premium in order to do so. Consumer hedging will, of course, work in the opposite direction. None the less, it is probably true that in 'ideal' conditions as to supply and demand a modest backwardation should be expected. Both backwardation and contango may show peaks or troughs for various dates within the forward trading period for which they are expressed. They do not necessarily progress in a straight line from cash to three months.

balance of payments
A summary of the international transactions of a country over a period of time including commodity and service transactions, capital transactions, and gold movements.

Banque Centrale de Compensation (BCC)
The clearer of the commodities futures contracts for the account and on behalf of MATIF S.A.

bar chart
A technical analysis chart that graphs the high, low, opening and settlement prices for a specific trading session over a given period of time. A vertical line on the graph shows the period high at the top, period low at the bottom extent. A small mark on the left hand side of this line shows the open price and a small mark out to the right shows the period close.

bargain
A deal made on, or subject to, the rules of the London Stock Exchange. It does not imply that there is a special price.

barrier option
There are various forms of barrier option. It is a path dependent option that becomes cancelled, or alternatively becomes activated, if the underlying asset reaches a certain level (out-strike, in-strike). This is regardless of where the underlying is trading at maturity. It is usually presented as a European option until, or from, the time the underlying asset reaches the barrier price. The following are the four main types. Up-and-out options are puts that become cancelled if the underlying rises above a certain level. Up-and-in options are worthless unless the underlying goes above a certain price whereupon it becomes a normal put option. Down-and-out options are calls that become cancelled if the underlying falls below a certain price, while down-and-ins are activated only when the underlying asset price falls to a certain level. Knock-in options are where the holder's ability to exercise is activated if the value of the underlying reaches a specified level, and a knock-out option is where the holder's ability to exercise is cancelled if the value of the underlying reaches a specified level. In all cases, the expiry date may be fixed until, or from the time, the underlying reaches the barrier price. Because of the potential cancellation of the contract, barrier options are cheaper than standard options and attractive to buyers who do not want to pay premium. In exchange for the relative cheapness, holders must take a view on the risk they can accept should the underlying reach a certain level. A hedger could buy an up-and-out put with an exercise price of 100 and a cancellation level of 120. If the asset falls to below 100 the option is exercised, and if it goes to 120 the option is cancelled (but, of course, the holder has no need to hedge the asset anymore). The holder needs to negotiate a trigger level high enough to make subsequent falls below the exercise price unlikely. Barrier options are also known as *limit options* or *trigger options*.

barrier price
The in-strike or out-strike price that activates or de-activates a barrier op-

tion. Some contracts require the barrier price only to be touched, others to be breached.

Basel Stock Exchange
Located in Basel, Switzerland, it lists contracts on equities, equity indices, Swiss government bonds and short-term interest rates.

basis
The difference between the current cash price and the futures price of the same financial instrument or commodity. It is normally calculated as cash price minus the futures price. A positive number indicates a futures discount (backwardation) and a negative number, a futures premium (contango). Unless otherwise specified, the price of the nearby futures contract month is generally used to calculate the basis. In physical markets, basis will also be affected by the location of the cash market, so the basis of wheat in Chicago compared with CBOT wheat future, and wheat in Europe compared with this contract will differ due to shipping, insurance and carry charges. *See also* **carry basis** and **value basis**.

basis grade
The grade of a commodity used as the standard of the futures contract.

basis order
See **contingent order**.

basis point
1/100th of one percentage point.

basis price
Agreed price between buyer and seller of an option at which the option may be taken up. Also called a *strike (or striking) price*, or an *exercise price*.

basis quote
Offer/sale of cash commodity as a difference above or below a futures price.

basket option
An option that gives the holder the right to buy or sell a basket of assets (usually currencies) against a base asset (currency).

BBA
British Bankers Association.

BBAISR
See **British Bankers' Association Interest Settlement Rate.**

BBF
See **Bolsa Brasileira de Futuros.**

BCC
Banque Centrale de Compensation. It clears the commodities futures contracts for the account and on behalf of MATIF SA.

bear
A person expecting a decline in prices.

bear cylinder (options)
A bear spread composed of a short put, long call and short underlying asset, it may also be referred to as a *fence*. It is a way of hedging the underlying asset. Gains and losses are limited. *See also* **cylinder.**

bear market
A market in which prices are declining.

bear rotated cylinder (options)
An options strategy that has the same expiry profile as a short synthetic future (split strike) but involves a short position in the underlying asset. It is composed of a short underlying asset plus a bull spread in options, comprised of either puts or calls. The centre section is a flat area hedging the asset price.

bear spread (futures)
In most commodities and financial instruments, the term refers to selling the nearby contract month, and buying the deferred contract, to profit from a change in the price relationship.

bear spread (options)
This strategy offers profits if the market falls slightly. If it is thought that the market is more likely to fall than to rise it offers profits at lower cost than a put option. It may be constructed from a short put at one exercise price, and a long put at a slightly higher exercise price in which case it is a long position. Equally calls may be used in place of puts, a short call, and a long call at a higher exercise price. The profile is the same but in this case a short position results. (The long components may also be reproduced synthetically). The profits and losses are capped off, with the maximum profit at or below the lower exercise price. The maximum loss is limited. The long

position holder expects the underlying to fall and volatility to rise, while the short position holder foresees a falling asset price and falling volatility. If the market is between the two exercise prices there is no time decay effect. Below this, profits increase at the fastest rate with time, and above the higher exercise price, it is losses that increase at the maximum rate with time. The expiry profile is flat, in profit, up to the low exercise price, falling to the higher exercise price, and then flat in loss as the underlying rises above that. A position composed of calls gives a maximum profit equal to short premium income less long premium cost. A position composed of puts gives a maximum loss equal to short premium income less long premium cost. *See also* **bull spread, bull cylinder** and **bear cylinder**.

bed and breakfast
A transaction where shares are sold one day and bought back the next in order to realize a capital gain or loss for tax purposes.

bed spread
The spread obtained from US Treasury bill and eurodollar futures. This is a trade based on quality margins.

BEF
Standard foreign exchange code for Belgian franc(s).

Belfox
See **Belgian Futures and Options Exchange**.

Belgian Futures and Options Exchange (Belfox)
Located in Brussels, Belfox lists contracts on equities, stock indices and Belgian government bonds.

Bermuda option
An option that is part-way between an American and a European option. Typically, it can be exercised on a number of predetermined occasions as stated in the option contract. It is a limited exercise or quasi-American option.

best execution
A principle concept or trading ethic which demands that brokers must always afford their clients total priority and the most advantageous transaction price available at the time of executing clients' orders.

best orders
These are buy or sell orders executed by the broker at what is considered to be the best price.

beta (or beta coefficient)
A statistical measurement of the relationship between the risk of an individual stock or stock portfolio and the risk of the overall market. The beta of a stock or portfolio measures the volatility of that stock or portfolio relative to the volatility of the overall market.

better-of-two-assets option
An option that pays out on the better performing of two underlying assets, for example, one that pays out the better performing of two stock indices.

BFI
Baltic Freight Index of voyage freight rates. It is composed of 14 representative dry bulk cargo freight rates averaged and weighted according to a predetermined formula.

BFr
Textual abbreviation for Belgian franc(s).

bid
An indication of willingness, made at a given moment, to buy a futures or options contract, or other asset, at a specific price.

bid into offers
An undesirable situation in open outcry markets where an intending buyer quotes a bid into a price level that is already declared as a valid offer, thus causing confusion as to the identity of the valid counterparty.

bid price
The price or yield on a security at which a purchaser will buy it. Some exchanges display such prices marked with a (B).

Big Bang
The changes in the UK Stock Exchange that took place on 27 October 1986. These included the introduction of the SEAQ screen-based quotation system and new regulations. It does not include the introduction of the Financial Services Act.

big figure
A trading term meaning the part of the contract price which is the least

significant in terms of quotation movement. Paradoxically, it is invariably the most significant in terms of contract value, e.g. in gilts valued at 105 and 12/32nds, 105 or even 5 would be termed the big figure.

binary option
See **digital option**.

binomial option pricing model
An approach to pricing options based upon a binomial tree.

Black-Derman-Toy option pricing model
A model for pricing interest rate options. It has no mean reversion and no analytical solution for European options.

Black options pricing model
A model for evaluating European options on futures contracts.

Black-Scholes options pricing model
A model for evaluating European options on non-dividend paying equity.

block order
An order for a standardized number of futures or options contracts. For example, OMLX defines a block order as ten contracts although this number is subject to change.

BM&F
See **Bolsade Mercadorias & Futuros Exchange**.

board official
A member of exchange staff appointed to ensure orderly trading on the floor.

Board of Trade Clearing Corporation
An independent corporation that settles all trades made at the Chicago Board of Trade acting as a guarantor for all trades cleared by it, reconciles all clearing member firm accounts each day to ensure that all gains have been credited and all losses have been collected, and sets and adjusts clearing member firm margins for changing market conditions. Also referred to as *The Clearing Corporation*. *See* **clearing house**.

board order
See **market if touched**.

Bodurtha and Courtadon option pricing model
A model for American options on foreign currency.

Bolsa Brasileira de Futuros (BBF)
A former futures exchange in São Paulo, Brazil. It listed contracts on currencies, gold and stock indices. Now absorbed into the Bolsade Mercadorias & Futuros Exchange.

Bolsade Mercadorias & Futuros Exchange (BM&F)
Located in São Paulo, Brazil, the BM&F lists contracts on cattle, coffee, gold, currencies, stock indices and CDs.

Bolsa de Valores do Rio de Janeiro (BVRJ)
A former exchange in Rio de Janeiro, Brazil. It listed equity options. Now absorbed into the Bolsade Mercadorias & Futuros Exchange.

Bolsa Mercantil & de Futuros
A former futures exchange in São Paulo, Brazil. It listed Treasuries, CDs, currencies, stock index, gold, livestock, coffee and soybeans. Now absorbed into the Bolsade Mercadorias & Futuros Exchange.

bond
An evidence of indebtedness. Usually in the form of a fixed-interest security (but could also be floating-rate). It will pay a coupon usually semi-annually or annually and have a maturity date when the face value of the bond is paid.

bond contract (futures and options)
See **long-term interest rate contract** and **long-term interest rate futures**.

bond warrant
See **debt warrant, warrants**.

bonus issue
See **capitalization issue**.

book-entry securities
Electronically-recorded securities that include each creditor's name, address, Social Security or tax identification number, and amount loaned, (i.e., no certificates are issued to bond holders, instead, the transfer agent electronically credits interest payments to each creditor's bank account on a designated date).

book transfer
Transfer of title to buyer without physical movement of product.

booking the basis
A forward pricing sales arrangement in which cash price is determined either by the buyer or seller within a specified time. At that time, the previously agreed basis is applied to the then current futures quotation.

booth
On open outcry exchanges, a floor member's trading centre and communications terminal.

borrower option
Cap on a single-period FRA.

borrowing
Buying cash on a nearby date and re-selling further forward. Both transactions are done at the same time and with the same counterparty, at prices and for dates agreed at the outset. Borrowers pay a premium if they borrows into a backwardation, and receive a premium should they borrow into a contango.

Boston option
A forward with an optional exit. *See* **break forward**.

bottom reversal day
A technical analysis term used to indicate that a new low in a downtrend is followed by a higher close on the same day, indicating a market move to an uptrend.

Bovespa index
See **São Paulo Stock Exchange Bovespa Index**.

box[1]
See **option box**.

box[2]
A similar term to **booth** above, but commonly a larger and more discreet facility on the London Commodity Exchange and IPE, for example.

brand
All metals deliverable on an exchange, for example the LME, must be of a brand registered as 'good delivery' by the exchange. Brands, of which there

may be many produced to different specifications and of different qualities by any given smelter or refiner are as a rule identifiable by some distinguishing mark.

BRC
Standard foreign exchange code for Brazilian cruzeiro(s).

break
A rapid and sharp price decline.

breakaway gap
A chart feature that is a gap that indicates the beginning of a new trend. It occurs on heavy volume in the direction of the trend and is not filled by minor reversals.

breakeven point
The underlying price at which a given options strategy is neither profitable nor unprofitable. For call options, it is the exercise price plus the premium. For put options, it is the exercise price minus the premium.

break forward
A forward contract which the purchaser can break at a predetermined rate. This allows advantage to be taken of any favourable rate movements. It usually relates to currencies. It is the terminology used by Midland Bank but it also known as a *Boston option, cancellable forward* and a *forward break*.

Brent Index
The cash price index for North Sea Brent crude oil, as calculated by the IPE.

British Bankers' Association Interest Settlement Rate
The rate used by LIFFE to mark-to-market daily and to settle its three-month interest rate contracts.

broadening formation
A chart reversal pattern that occurs in confused market conditions. The trendline and record line diverge and a failure to bounce back from one to the other indicates a break in the direction of the last line touched.

broad tape
Term commonly applied to news wires carrying price and background information on securities and commodities markets, in contrast to the exchanges' own price transmission wires.

broker
A person paid a fee or commission for executing buy or sell orders of a customer. In futures trading, the term may refer to (1) floor broker - a person who actually executes orders on the trading floor of an exchange; (2) account executive, associated person, registered commodity representative or customer's man - the person who deals with customers in the offices of futures commission merchants; and (3) the futures commission merchant.

brokerage fee
The fee charged by a broker for execution of a transaction. The fee may be a flat amount or a percentage. *See also* **commission fee**.

BSI
The British Standards Institute. The official body in the United Kingdom for laying down standards as to purity and methods for sampling and assaying metals as well as other standards.

BTAN
French government *Bons du Trésor à Intérêt Annuel Normalisé*, Treasury notes with original maturities of 2 and 5 years. Coupons are payable annually.

BTP
Buoni del Tesoro Poliennali, or Italian Treasury bond.

bucketing
Directly or indirectly taking the opposite side of a customer's order into the handling broker's own account or into an account in which he or she has an interest, without execution on an exchange.

bulge
A rapid advance in prices.

bull
A person expecting a rise in prices.

bull cylinder (options)
A bull spread composed of a long put, short call, and the underlying asset, it is also called a *fence*. Gains and losses are limited and it may be considered a way of hedging the underlying asset. *See also* **bear cylinder**.

bullion
Gold in bars or ingots assaying at least 995 fine.

bull market
A market in which prices are rising.

bull rotated cylinder (options)
An options strategy that has the same expiry profile as a long synthetic future (split strike) but involves a long position in the underlying asset. It is composed of a long underlying asset plus a bear spread in options, comprised of either calls or puts. The centre section is a flat area hedging the asset price.

bull spread (futures)
In most commodities and financial instruments, the term refers to buying the nearby month, and selling the deferred month, to profit from the change in the price relationship.

bull spread (options)
The most popular bullish trade it offers profits if the underlying asset rises slightly. If it is thought that the market is more likely to rise than to fall it offers profits at lower cost than a call option. It may be constructed from a long call at one exercise price, and a short call at a slightly higher exercise price thus making it a long position. Equally puts may be used in place of calls, a long put and a short put at a higher exercise price resulting in a short position. The profile is the same. (The short components may also be reproduced synthetically). The profits and losses are capped off, with the maximum profit at or above the higher exercise price. The maximum loss is limited. A long position holder expects the underlying to rise, and also sees volatility as likely to rise, while a short position holder expects the underlying to rise but volatility to fall. If the market is between the two exercise prices there is low time decay effect. Above this profits increase at the fastest rate with time, and below the lower exercise price it is losses that increase at the maximum rate with time. The expiry profile is flat, at a loss, up to the low exercise price, rising to the higher exercise price, and then flat in profit above that. A position composed of calls gives a maximum loss equal to short premium income less long premium cost. A position composed of puts gives a maximum profit equal to short premium income less long premium cost. *See also* **bull cylinder** and **bear cylinder**.

Buoni del Tesoro Poliennali (BTP)
Italian Treasury bond.

Bunds
Bundesrepublik Deutschland bonds or German government bonds, usually

issued with maturities of ten years at close to par. They pay an annual coupon.

buoyant
A market in which prices have a tendency to rise easily.

butterfly spread (futures)
A spread taken out in two adjacent maturity contracts together with an opposite spread in the latter contract and the next maturity contract. Consider the position at the beginning of the year. If the spot price is 100, March futures 110, June futures 115 and July futures 130 it may be considered that June futures are mispriced. If this view is taken then to take advantage of a June futures price rise relative to March one should sell March and buy June. To take advantage of a price rise relative to July one should buy June and sell July. In total, one would have a short March, two long June and short July position. This is a butterfly spread. It is the placing of two inter-delivery spreads in opposite directions with the centre delivery month common to both spreads. Should be unwound if one's view comes correct.

butterfly (options)
See **long butterfly** and **short butterfly**.

button
A general term on UK exchanges to describe a trainee trader.

buyer
A trader originating a bid or accepting a counterparty offer.

buyer's call
A term that generally applies to cotton. A purchase of a specified quantity of a specific grade of a commodity at a fixed number of points above or below a specified delivery month futures price with the buyer allowed a period of time to fix the price either by purchasing a future for the account of the seller or telling the seller when the price should be fixed.

buyer in
The trader currently bidding best market price or accepting market offers at the end of a call-over period. The trader may claim priority for later sale orders. It only may apply in markets that operate a call-over system.

buyer over
A bidder who is still unsatisfied (i.e., still calling a bid) at the close of a

call-over period of trading. An unsatisfied buyer who may then claim priority. It only may apply in markets that operate a call-over system. *See* **seller over**.

buy in
Making a purchase to cover a previous sale, often called *covering*.

buying basis
Difference between cost of a cash commodity and a future sold as a hedge. *See* **selling basis**.

buying hedge
See **purchasing hedge**.

buy on close
To buy at the end of a trading session at a price within the closing range.

buy on opening
To buy at the beginning of a trading session at a price within the opening range.

buy-writes
Strategies that involve the purchase of stock and the simultaneous writing of call options against it. They reduce the cost of the stock purchase to the extent of the premium received.

BVRJ
See **Bolsa de Valores do Rio de Janeiro**.

C

C$
Textual abbreviation for Canadian dollar(s).

cab
Cabinet bid.

cabinet bid
A facility enabling holders of out-of-the-money options to close their positions for a nominal sum per contract to establish a tax loss. No clearing fees are chargeable on this transaction.

cable
Spot dollar-sterling foreign exchange rate.

CAC-40
The principal French equity index, Compagniedes Agents de Change-40. Futures trade on Matif and options on MONEP.

CAD
Standard foreign exchange code for Canadian dollar(s).

calendar spread
Also called *diagonal spread*. See **horizontal spread**.

call
A period at the opening and the close of some futures markets in which the price for each futures contract is established by auction.

call chairman
An independent exchange official (for example at the LCE) who regularly presides at market calls, (the exchange name for two-way commodity auctions).

call feature
The ability of the issuer of a bond or other instrument to redeem it prior to maturity. This will occur with dual-dated bonds, where they may be redeemed at any time between the two dates.

call option
An option that gives the holder the right (but not the obligation) in exchange for payment of a premium, to buy the underlying asset at a specific price, and obligates the seller to sell the underlying asset at a specific price, should the option be exercised. If the option is an option on a future the holder will obtain a long futures position if exercise takes place and the writer a short futures position, both at the exercise price.

call-over
The pre-market activity and challenges, to estimate a markets likely opening levels and movement; prices quoted at such time are indicative only.

call ratio backspread
This position is the opposite to that of a call ratio spread. It is a bear call spread with a further purchased call at the higher exercise price, or a long straddle with lower cost traded off against reduced profits from a downwards movement. It is normally taken on when the market stands near the higher exercise price and is likely to become more volatile or move upwards. It is formed from a short call at the low exercise price with two long calls at the higher exercise price, resulting in an expiry profile of a flat line, a falling line from the lower to higher exercise price, and then a rising line, plotted against the underlying asset. It may also be constructed synthetically using a short put at a lower exercise price, two long calls at the higher price, and a short underlying asset. Downside profit is limited to the net premium income whilst upside potential if the market rises is open ended. Losses are incurred if the underlying asset stays at the higher exercise price. Time decay is greatest and works against the holder here, but is favourable if the underlying asset is below the lower exercise price.

call ratio spread
The call ratio spread is a bull call spread with a further sold call at the higher exercise price, or a cheaper short straddle with downside risk reduced. It is a trade on the precision of pricing. It thus forms a profile of a flat line to the first exercise price, an ascending line to the second exercise price, and then a downward sloping line thereafter, as the underlying asset price rises. It is used when the underlying asset market is near the lower exercise price and a slight rise is expected, but not a sharp price rise because unlimited losses could then be incurred. The selling of the additional call compared with the bull spread results in a low cost strategy in exchange for this extra risk. More than two calls may be sold to reduce cost further, but seldom more than three sold because of the upside risk. It is important to realize that the position is net short of calls and that it may be advisable to have sufficient cover in place. The position may also be con-

structed from a long put at the lower exercise price, short calls at the higher price, and a long underlying asset. All constructions are done to initial delta neutrality. Loss is limited to the net cost of the position if the underlying falls if constructed from calls, but is open-ended if the underlying rises, in proportion to the number of short positions. Time decay works in the holder's favour at the higher exercise price, and against the holder at the lower price.

call spread (options)
A call purchase reduced by the sale of another call at a higher exercise price. This is a long bull spread. Advantageous if the purchaser thinks that there is only limited upside potential.

call table top
Similar to a call ratio spread except that the short call options are at two different exercise prices leaving a flat part between them. The expiry profile is thus flat, near to break-even, rising, flat in profit, then descending into loss.

cancel former order
An order which allows a client to enter a new order, as a substitution for, or an amendment to, some aspect of a previous order.

cancellable forward
Goldman Sachs name for a **break forward**.

cancelling order
An order that deletes a customer's previous order. Also a *closing order*. See **closing purchase, closing sale**.

candlestick chart
A technical analysis chart that contains the same information as a bar chart but which is visually quite different. A vertical rectangle is drawn with the daily open and close at the top and bottom, and the high as a spike off the top and low as a spike off the bottom. If the close is higher than the open then the rectangle is left empty. If the open is higher than the close it is inked in solid.

cap
An option agreement that puts a ceiling or cap on an interest rate or on rates of reference in foreign exchange or equity markets. The cap is a strip of interest rate guarantees. If, on prescribed reference dates, a standard rate is above a rate agreed between the seller of the cap and the buyer, then the

seller pays the buyer the extra interest costs until the next reference date. Borrowers at a floating-rate (usually six-month Libor plus a certain amount) can thus cap their floating-rate borrowing and ensure that they pay no more than a certain maximum amount. Caps allow borrowers to take advantage of falling rates but do not expose them to high rates. They are priced as the sum total of the cost of the individual period options. They are most useful for highly leveraged companies, and are sold by those who believe rates will fall. *See also* **compound option**.

capitalization issue
An issue of shares to shareholders made in proportion to their existing holdings. The shares are issued free of charge, being funded by a transfer from a company's reserves. Also known as a *bonus* or *scrip issue*.

caplet
One of the interim period cap components in a multi-period interest rate cap agreement.

capped option
An option where the holder's potential profit from a favourable change in the underlying asset is capped off at a specific limited amount.

caption
An option to buy a cap. A form of compound option giving the holder the right, but not the obligation, to enter into a cap contract at a predetermined rate on a predetermined date. As such, these are options on options and provide a relatively cheap way of leveraging in to a more expensive option. This is especially useful where a company is unsure how much interest rate exposure it will have. It might have to borrow money for a project on which it is bidding—the knowledge that it can get a fixed borrowing cost allows a more precise, and perhaps cheaper, bid. If the bid is unsuccessful, it is spared the cost of the option itself and may be able to trade back the caption.

card
A pit trader's hand-held stationery on which transactions are noted, usually in a standard form of shorthand code.

carload or car
The load of a railroad freight car; a loose, quantitative term sometimes used to describe a contract, e.g. 'a car of potatoes'.

carry
The (positive or negative) return on a trader's book net of financing costs.

The cost of holding an asset from one period to another including the cost of borrowing to purchase it.

carry (LME)
Contract of purchase or sale of a specific quantity of metal for one settlement or prompt date coupled with a contract for sale or, as the case may be, purchase of the same tonnage of the same metal between the same parties for a more distant prompt date.

carry basis
The difference between the cash price and the fair futures price. It reflects the net carrying cost. Actual basis is the sum of carry basis and value basis.

carrying
General term covering both borrowing and lending.

carrying broker
A member of a commodity exchange, usually a commission house broker, through whom other brokers or customers elect to clear all or part of their trades.

carrying charge
For physical commodities such as grains and metals, the cost of storage space, insurance, and finance charges incurred by holding a physical commodity. In financial futures markets it refers to the differential between the yield on a cash instrument and the cost of funds necessary to buy the instrument. Also referred to as *cost of carry* or *carry*.

carrying charge market
A market in contango or with futures at a premium to cash.

carry-over
Grain and oilseed commodities not consumed during the marketing year and remaining in storage at year's end. These stocks are 'carried over' into the next marketing year and added to the stocks produced during that crop year.

cash and carry
An arbitrage where the simultaneous purchase of a cash instrument or commodity is made with borrowed money, and the item sold through a futures contract. An arbitrage profit is made if the futures price is higher than its theoretical price, that is if the premium of futures over spot price exceeds the cost of carry.

cash commodity
An actual physical commodity someone is buying or selling, e.g., soybeans, corn, gold, silver, etc. Also referred to as *actuals* or *physicals*.

cash contract
A sales agreement for either immediate or future delivery of the actual product.

cash forward sale
See **forward contract**.

cash instrument
A financial instrument or commodity.

cash market
A physical place or telephone market where people buy and sell the actual underlying instruments or commodities, i.e., foreign exchange, money, equity or bond markets, oil spot market, grain elevator, bank, etc. *See* **spot** and **forward contract**.

cash or physical market
Market for immediate delivery of and payment for commodities.

cash price
The price in the market-place for actual cash or spot commodities to be delivered via customary market channels, the spot price.

cash settlement[1]
Transactions generally involving index-based futures contracts that are settled in cash, based on the actual value of the index on the last trading day, in contrast to those that specify the delivery of a commodity or financial instrument.

cash settlement[2]
The delivery of securities against payment where the settlement date is the same as the trade date. The term is typically used in the US money markets. Known as *same-day settlement* in the UK.

cash settlement[3]
Delivery of securities for payment the day after the trade date, the next business day. This is the normal form of settlement in the UK gilt market.

cash today (LME)
In relation to the period between 17.00 house on one business day and the close of the first morning ring trading session on the next business day, the first settlement business day after that business day. An exchange contract made before commencement of the second ring on any business day to be settled on the next settlement business day after that day on the LME.

CBOE
See **Chicago Board Options Exchange**.

CBOT
See **Chicago Board of Trade**.

CCC
Commodity Credit Corporation. A government-owned corporation established in 1933 to assist American agriculture. Major operations include price support programs, supply control and foreign sales programs for agricultural commodities.

CD
Certificate of deposit. See **certificate of deposit**.

CDR
Collateralized Depository Receipt.

Cedel
Centrale de Livraison de Valeurs mobiles. A clearing system for the eurocurrency market, based in Luxembourg and owned by several banks. It operates like Euroclear.

certificate of deposit (CD)
A tradeable time deposit with a specific maturity evidenced by a certificate.

certificated or certified stocks
Stocks of a commodity that have been inspected and found to be a quality deliverable against futures contracts, stored at the delivery points designated as regular or acceptable for delivery by the commodity exchange. In grain, called 'stocks in deliverable position'.

C&F
Cost and freight. A contractual term indicating that the price to the buyer includes transit costs, but not insurance.

CFTC
The Commodity Futures Trading Commission.

CFO
Cancel former order.

CHAPS
Clearing Houses Automated Payment System (The UK Banker's Clearing House).

Charm[1]
The London Stock Exchange's trade checking and confirmation system.

charm[2]
A measure of the change in delta as time passes and prices remain the same.

charting
The use of charts to analyse market behaviour and anticipate future price movements. Those who use charting as a trading method plot volume; and open interest. Two basic price charts are bar charts, close price, tick charts and point-and-figure charts. *See* **technical analysis**.

cheap
Colloquialism implying that a security, commodity, or derivative is underpriced.

cheapest to deliver
The actual bond or particular cash debt instrument which provides the greatest profit or the least loss when delivered against a futures contract on a notional instrument, e.g., long gilt or T-bond futures.

cherry picking
An illegal practice whereby traders assign advantageous trades to their account to the disadvantage of their clients. The antithesis of best execution.

Chicago Board of Trade (CBOT)
A US exchange which lists futures and options for a large variety of financial and agricultural contracts, together with gold and silver.

Chicago Board Options Exchange (CBOE)
A US exchange which lists options on equity, bonds, indices and interest rates.

Chicago Mercantile Exchange (CME)
A US exchange which lists contracts on currencies, currency cross rates, S&P 500, Nikkei 225, eurodollar deposits, 13-week US T-bills, cattle, chickens, live hogs, pork bellies, etc.

CHF
Standard foreign exchange code for Swiss franc(s).

CHIPS
Clearing House Interbank Payments System. The system of electronic bank transfers used in the USA.

choice (foreign exchange and currency deposit markets)
A principal is a buyer or seller at one price. The bid and offer price are the same.

chooser option
An option that offers the holder the choice during a pre-determined period to designate the option to be a call or a put. These options, whilst similar to straddles, are cheaper because the holder must decide prior to expiry whether to have a call or a put. They provide a useful vehicle for a person anticipating information but unable to determine as yet whether it will have a beneficial or adverse effect on the underlying asset.

Christmas tree
A type of ratio vertical spread where options are sold at two or more different exercise prices. This includes **table tops**.

churning
Unethical behaviour involving excessive trading which permits the broker to derive a commission while disregarding the best interests of the customer.

CIF
Cost, insurance and freight (included in the price). A contractual term indicating that the price quoted to the buyer includes transit costs and insurance.

class of option
Options pertaining to the same underlying stock.

clean deposit
A 'clean' or 'straight' deposit is one where there is no CD involved e.g. "I pay for clean (or straight) threes" or "I lend clean (or straight) sixes".

clean price
The price of a bond exclusive of accrued interest.

clear
The process by which a clearing house maintains records of all trades and settles margin flow on a daily mark-to-market basis for its clearing members.

clearances
Aggregate shipments of a commodity made by sea on a specified date.

clearing
The procedure through which the clearing house or association becomes buyer to each seller of a futures contract, and seller to each buyer, and assumes responsibility for protecting buyers and sellers from loss by assuring the financial integrity of each contract open on its books.

clearing agent
A clearing member of an exchange clearing house that may clear the trades of non-clearing members.

clearing bureau
An intermediary organization which provides accounting, position control and trade analysis facilities, by interfacing on behalf of a broking or trading organization; the exchange and the official clearing house. A bureau does not offer any formal guarantee to the performance of transactions.

clearing corporation
See **Board of Trade Clearing Corporation**.

clearing fee
A sum charged by the clearing house. All trades executed on the floor must be registered and held with a clearing member.

clearing house
An agent, or in some cases a wholly-owned subsidiary organization of a derivative exchange. Its responsibilities are to administer registered trades on behalf of exchange members through the principle process of counter-party substitution (it becomes the buyer to every seller and the seller to every buyer); position and risk management through the process of margin

call and collection; the profit and loss accounting process, normally handled through special banking arrangements; and the process of liquidation by counter trade on the market or by physical delivery. Throughout the entire cycle of transaction management, the most important single factor of the clearing house operation is the timing and quality of the guarantee of transaction performance that it is able to offer the exchange and its members. Clearing houses cover both floor trades and automated trades.

clearing margin
Financial safeguards to ensure that clearing members (usually companies or corporations) perform on their customers' open futures and options contracts. Clearing margins are distinct from customer margins that individual buyers and sellers of futures and options contracts are required to deposit with brokers. *See* **customer margin**.

clearing member
A member of an exchange clearing house. Clearing members are responsible for the financial commitments of customers that clear through their firm. All trades of a non-clearing member must be registered and eventually settled through a clearing member. All trades on a floor must be registered and held with a clearing member.

client
A person using the services of a broker or agent *See* **counterparty**.

client account
Any individual or entity being serviced by an agent (broker) for a commission. Servicing generally includes advice, accounting, and order execution. A customer's business must be distinguished from the brokers principal inhouse business and may be in a physically segregated account at the client's option.

client agreement
A legal document meeting the requirements of the relevant self-regulating organization and exchange entered into between the broker and the client and setting out the conditions of their relationship.

client contract
A contract between a clearing member and any person other than another clearing member or a contract between a member who is not a clearing member and any other person.

client option
An option where either grantor or taker or each of them is not a clearing member.

close, the
The period at the end of the trading session officially designated by the exchange during which all transactions are considered made 'at the close'.

close out
A purchase or sale transaction leaving a trader with a zero net position.

closing order
A closing order is an order to buy or sell at a specified price that is within the closing range of a contract. It need not be the exact closing price but must be within the range. *See also* **closing purchase** and **closing sale**.

closing price (or range)
The price (or price range) recorded in the trading place in the final movements of a day's trade that are officially designated as the 'close'. *See also* **settlement price**.

closing purchase
A purchase of a derivative position on an exchange that is exactly the same as a sold position already held. This leaves a net zero position with the clearing house.

closing range
A range of prices at which buy and sell transactions took place during the market close.

closing sale
A sale of derivative position that cancels an open purchased position.

CME
See **Chicago Mercantile Exchange**.

code of conduct
The trading procedures and etiquette of an exchange or market.

Coffee, Sugar & Cocoa Exchange, Inc. (CSCE)
Located in New York, it lists contracts on coffee, sugar, cocoa, cheese and nonfat dry milk.

collar (options[1])
This is the simultaneous purchase of a cap and sale of a floor, used with interest rates. It is based on an expectation of rising rates. The premium income from the sold floor reduces the cost of purchasing the cap. Clearly the cap exercise price will be higher than the floor exercise price and the expiry profile will be comparable to that of a synthetic split strike future or rotated cylinder. If the premiums are virtually the same a zero cost collar results. If rates fall the purchaser of the collar will have to pay the difference between the floor and prevailing rates. It thus establishes a desired band in which buyers of the collar want their interest rate costs to be held.

collar (options[2])
A fence or cylinder used to hedge an interest rate position. *See* **bull cylinder** and **bear cylinder**.

collateralized depository receipt (CDR)
A financial instrument which represents GNMA certificates held in safekeeping.

colour
A measure of the rate of change of gamma as time passes and prices stay the same.

combination
An options strategy that is the same as a strangle but the calls and puts employed are both out-of-the-money. Also any options strategy formed from calls and puts.

COMEX
See **Commodity Exchange Inc.**

combo
A bought put with a short call at a higher strike price. In other words a synthetic short future with a split strike price.

commercial
A company that merchandises or processes cash commodities.

commercial grain stocks
Domestic grain in store in public and private elevators at important markets and grain afloat in port.

commercial paper
Short-term promissory notes issued in bearer form by large corporations, with maturities ranging from 5 to 270 days. Since the notes are unsecured, the commercial paper market generally is dominated by large corporations with impeccable credit ratings.

commission[1]
The one-time fee charged by a broker to a customer when a position is liquidated either by offset or delivery. Commissions are negotiable in the UK.

Commission[2]
The CFTC.

commission fee
A fee charged by a broker for executing a transaction. Also referred to as *brokerage fee* (US).

commission house
A company which trades on behalf of clients for a commission. The commission house only handles clients' business and does not trade on its own account. *See also* **futures commission merchant (US)**.

commodity
An article of commerce or a product that can be used for commerce. In a narrow sense, products traded on an authorized commodity exchange. The types of commodities include agricultural products, metals, petroleum, foreign currencies and financial instruments and indices.

Commodity Board
US legal term for an exchange registered under the Commodity Exchange Act.

Commodity Credit Corporation (CCC)
A branch of the US Department of Agriculture, established in 1933, that supervises the government's farm loan and subsidy programs.

Commodity Exchange Act 1936 (US)
The US legislation that led to the licensing of US exchanges and the formation of the CFTC.

Commodity Exchange Inc. (COMEX)
Located in New York, it lists contracts on precious and base metals.

Commodity Futures Trading Commission (CFTC)
A federal regulatory agency established under the Commodity Futures Trading Commission Act, as amended in 1974, that oversees futures trading in the US. The commission is comprised of five commissioners, one of whom is designated as chairman, all appointed by the President subject to Senate confirmation, and is independent of all cabinet departments. It administers the Commodity Exchange Act.

commodity pool
An enterprise in which funds contributed by a number of persons are combined for the purpose of trading futures contracts or commodity options.

commodity pool operator (CPO)
Individuals or firms in businesses similar to investment trusts or syndicates that solicit or accept funds, securities or property for trading in commodity futures contracts. (US)

commodity price index
Index, or average, of commodity price movements.

commodity trading adviser (CTA)
A person who, for compensation or profit, directly or indirectly advises others as to the value or the advisability of buying or selling futures contracts or commodity options. Advising indirectly includes exercising trading authority over a customer's account as well as providing recommendations through written publications or other media. (US)

commodity warrant
A warrant giving the holder the right to purchase a commodity. *See* **warrant**.

common stock
US term for ordinary share(s).

compliance
Action to comply with rules and regulations. A firm's department responsible for the maintenance and adherence to rules and regulations of a regulatory body or an exchange.

compound option
An option on an option. These have so far related mostly to interest rate option products such as caps (captions) and floors (floortions), but also to currencies. They provide hedging opportunities for corporates with contin-

gent interest rate or currency exposures. Premiums are priced off the underlying asset and not the underlying option, and if exercised can add as much as 50% to the overall premium cost. They are relatively expensive because their volatility is magnified by that of the underlying option. Consequently they are also used by speculators, since downside risk is limited to the premium whilst high volatility means very sharp price movements.

Computerized Trading Reconstruction (CTR) System
A Chicago Board of Trade computerized surveillance program that pinpoints in any trade the traders, the contract, the quantity, the price and the time of execution to the nearest minute.

condor
An option butterfly with a wider spread of exercise prices. *See* **long condor** and **short condor**.

confirmation
The process whereby, immediately following a transaction, the traders confirm the details of the trade.

congestion
In technical analysis, an area of repetitious and limited price fluctuations within a narrow trading range.

congestion at port
Ships are waiting to unload. This can cause sellers to reject the buyers nominated lifting time.

consideration
The monetary value of a UK equity transaction (number of shares times the price), exclusive of commission, stamp duty, etc.

consumer price index (CPI)
An index that measures the change in prices of a fixed basket of goods purchased by consumers. Most countries produce such data on a monthly basis. The US CPI is computed by the US Department of Commerce. It measures the change in prices of a fixed market basket of some 385 goods and services in the previous month. *See also* **retail price index**.

contango
A situation where prices are higher in the forward delivery months than in the nearby delivery month. Opposite of **backwardation**. Normally in evidence when supplies are adequate or in surplus. The contango reflects,

either wholly or in part, the costs of holding and financing. When the market is stable and in balance there is usually a premium which reflects prevailing short-term interest rates.

contingent order or basis order
An order which is dependent on the price of another contract month or another instrument or commodity.

contingent option
An option where the premium, while higher than usual, is only paid if the value of the underlying asset reaches a specified level. Also known as a *contingent premium option*.

contingent premium option
See **contingent option**.

continuation pattern
A chart pattern that indicates that the current direction of price movements will be maintained.

contract
A binding agreement to buy or sell a specified amount of a particular financial instrument or commodity. The contract details specify the financial instrument or show the amount and grade of the product and the date on which the contract will mature and become deliverable, if not previously liquidated.

contract admin. terms
The general terms of contract and delivery covering a derivative instrument.

contract code
The standard shortened form of contract reference used in trade reporting and trade matching.

contract for differences
A contract based upon the movement in value, rate of exchange or rate of interest between two or more cash or derivative instruments. Such contracts are usually subject to cash settlement as opposed to physical delivery or settlement to a specific market value.

contract grades
That which is deliverable on a futures contract. Basic contract grade is the

one deliverable at par. There may be more than one basic grade. *See* **deliverable grades**.

Contract Market
A Board of Trade designated by the Commodity Futures Trading Commission as a Contract Market for a specific commodity under the Commodity Exchange Act.

contract month(s)
The month(s) in which futures contracts may be satisfied by making or accepting a delivery.

contract note
A written form of confirmation from brokers to their clients carrying minimum details of trades effected to their orders and accounts, normally on a daily basis.

contract price
The price agreed between the parties at which a contract is entered into.

contract symbol
An alternative term for contract code.

contract trading volume
The total number of contracts traded in a financial instrument or commodity delivery month during a specified period of time, usually a day, month or year.

contract unit
The actual amount of a financial instrument or commodity designated in a given futures contract.

contract weights
Deliverable weights of contract as shown on warehouse receipts.

contra trade
An offsetting trade used most frequently to neutralize the effect and potential loss of an original trade executed erroneously.

controlled account
Any account for which trading is directed by someone other than the owner. *See also* **discretionary account**.

conventional option
See **traditional option**.

convergence
A term referring to cash and futures prices tending to come together (i.e., the basis approaches zero) as the futures contract nears expiration.

conversion
See **option conversion**.

conversion factor
A factor used to equate the price of bond and note futures contracts with the various cash bonds and notes eligible for delivery. *See* **price factor**.

convertible bond
A bond that may be converted into a company's equity (or into other bonds) at certain dates on prearranged terms. Convertible gilts similarly convert into other gilt stocks.

Copenhagen Stock Exchange & Guarantee Fund for Danish Options and Futures (FUTOP)
This Danish combination of exchange and clearing house (together as FUTOP) lists contracts on government and mortgage bonds, stock indices and equities.

corner
To corner is to secure such relative control of a commodity or security that its price can be manipulated. In the extreme situation, obtaining contracts requiring delivery of more commodities or securities than are available for delivery.

corporate bond
An instrument evidencing indebtedness of a corporation.

corporate local
Holders of this membership category are traders who are allowed to execute trades for their own account but whose authority to do so is dependent upon their employer's exchange membership as opposed to the individual being an exchange member in his or her own right.

corporate settlement (currency asset markets)
Settlement five business days after trade date in the US, but after one week in eurobond trading.

correlation coefficient
A statistical measurement of the degree of correlation between the price of a stock and the overall market. The correlation coefficient is expressed as an R^2 value ranging from zero for no correlation to 1.0 for perfect correlation.

cost of carry (or carry)
Costs incurred in warehousing a physical commodity including interest for purchase, storage and insurance. *See* **carrying charge**.

counterparty
A person or institution who forms the other side of a deal or agreement with a principal or other counterparty, *See* **client**.

counterparty risk
The theoretical exposure of one party to the risk that a trade counterparty might default or fail to deliver his or her obligations with no form of insurance or contract guarantee available to offset or mitigate such occurrence.

coupon
The rate of interest that a bond guarantees to pay, based on the bond's face value. This may be paid annually, semi-annually, or even more frequently in the case of FRNs.

cover
To purchase futures to offset a short position. To have in hand the physical commodity when a short futures sale is made, or to acquire the commodity that might be deliverable on a short sale.

covered call option
This is a short call option position where the writer holds the underlying asset. If exercised against the asset is surrendered to provide fulfilment of the contract. This reduces the risk of the position and changes the expiry profile to that of a short put option. Income is made if the underlying asset rises in price equivalent to the premium income. If the asset rises spectacularly it will be surrendered through exercise and such gains foregone. If the asset falls in value the option will not be exercised and the premium income retained, but since the asset itself is held it must be marked down in value. This is a strategy that can be followed by persons holding the underlying asset long term and believing that the market will not rise, as a means of adding extra income to a portfolio. Also called a *buy write*.

covered interest arbitrage
The arbitrage mechanism that prices currency futures and forwards. Inves-

tors in the UK could buy three-month Treasury bills and hence know the exact return they will make at maturity. Alternatively, they could take their investment capital and buy US dollars spot, invest in three-month US T-bills, and know what their dollar return in three months will be. The quoted futures or forward rates should show these two routes as giving an equal return when measured in either sterling or dollars. If this is not the case, then risk-free arbitrage profits can be generated by borrowing in one currency for three months, buying the other currency spot, investing in a three month financial instrument in that other currency, and selling that currency forward back into the borrowed currency.

covered option
A written option is said to be covered if it is matched by an opposing cash or futures position in the underlying asset, or by an opposing option position in the underlying asset, or by an opposing option position of specific characteristics.

covered warrant
A warrant issued by a company or securities house that enables the holder to buy shares in another company. It is referred to as *covered* because the issuer should have made arrangements to hold or obtain the underlying shares at the time the warrant may be exercised.

covered write
Sale of calls against an existing long options or long cash position. Also called a *buy write*.

Cox option pricing model
An equity call option pricing model that explicitly assumes a non-stationary variance of stock returns.

Cox-Ingersoll-Ross option pricing model
A model for pricing interest rate options. It does not guarantee consistency with the initial term structure, has mean reversion, analytic solution for European options.

Cox-Ross-Rubinstein (Binomial) model
A binomial-based option pricing model that values American options.

CPS
Clearing Processing System. Introduced by LIFFE and now extended to LCE and IPE.

crack spread
The spread obtained from buying futures on crude oil and selling futures on refined oil, that is to synthetically act like a refinery. Any combination of energy futures can be used, provided that the value of crude contracts is equivalent to the value of product contracts.

CRB
Commodity Research Bureau in the US.

credit box
See **option box**.

credit risk
The theoretical exposure of one party to the risk that any form of credit or loan, inherent or extended, to a counterparty in the conduct of its business may not be repaid or recovered by the expected or due date.

CREST
The Bank of England's system for stock exchange settlements currently under design as a successor to TALISMAN and a replacement for the failed TAURUS project.

crop (marketing) year
The time span from harvest to harvest for agricultural commodities. The crop marketing year varies slightly with each agricultural commodity, but tends to begin at harvest and end before the next year's harvest, e.g., the marketing year for soybeans begins September 1 and ends August 31. The futures contract month of November represents the first major new-crop marketing month, and the contract month of July represents the last major old-crop marketing month for soybeans.

crop reports
Reports compiled by the US Department of Agriculture on various agricultural commodities that are released throughout the year. Information in the reports includes estimates on planted acreage, yield, and expected production, as well as comparison of production from previous years.

cross-currency cap
A cap where the payout to the holder is the spread between two currency base rates (say sterling Libor and dollar Libor) minus a strike spread, when this exceeds zero. It can thus be considered as a strip of options on forward spread agreements.

cross/self trade
A deemed sale and purchase by a clearing member in the pit to and from himself for equal amounts of a contract of the same month at a single price.

cross-hedging
Hedging a cash commodity using a different but related futures contract when there is no futures contract for the cash commodity being hedged and the cash and futures markets follow similar price trends (e.g., using soybean meal futures to hedge fish meal).

cross-rate
In foreign exchange, the price of one currency in terms of another currency, not involving a quote against dollar or sterling, e.g., franc/yen.

cross trade/cross trading
A transaction in which the executing party is counterparty to his or her own offer and bid respectively. Such trades are primarily intended to allow brokers to match and register business that has originated from two independent client orders. In certain circumstances, particularly in very quiet and illiquid contracts, brokers may give effect to client orders by taking the opposite position to the clients onto their own house account. Exchanges will monitor this area of activity closely to ensure the principle of best execution is not prejudiced and, where practical, will require that brokers give opportunity for the market to participate in cross trades before allowing the brokers to complete their business. Thus a competitive element is maintained.

crowd
The market-makers and broker dealers at a particular pitch.

crush[1] (physical)
A commodity statistic normally released by a processor or trade association on a predetermined date and interval, declaring the tonnage of a given commodity (typically soya beans, cocoa or oil seeds) that has been processed over a given period of time.

crush[2]
The purchase of soybean futures (or cash soybeans) and the simultaneous sale of soybean oil and meal futures (or cash soybean oil and meal). This spread is used to minimize the financial risks of sudden increases in soybean costs and/or declining values of finished soybean oil and meal. It is synthetically to act like a soy bean crusher. Both contracts are available on the Chicago Board of Trade.

CSCE
See **Coffee, Sugar & Cocoa Exchange, Inc.**

ctd
See **cheapest to deliver.**

cum
Latin, meaning 'with'. Cum-dividend means a security is sold such that the buyer will obtain the next dividend or coupon. Similarly cum-capitalization, cum-rights. The opposite of ex. See also **ex.**

currency contract
A futures or options contract for a currency, quoted in terms of another. In London, the strength of the interbank OTC market has defeated attempts by its exchanges to maintain contracts. The major world currency futures market is the IMM Division of the Chicago Mercantile Exchange, while the premier options market is the Philadelphia Stock Exchange. On these markets the contract is for a fixed amount of non-US dollar currency (such as the British pound, Deutschemark, Swiss franc, etc.), quoted in US dollars. It is the dollar figure that will vary according to market sentiment. The seller of a futures contract will thus sell the contractual amount of the base currency in exchange for US dollars. Option premiums are expressed in dollars and strike prices are in dollars for exchange into a fixed amount of the contract currency.

currency convertible
A bond that includes a put feature together with a currency option. The currency option gives the holder the right to convert the currency of issue into another currency at a fixed exchange rate at redemption.

currency option
The option to buy or sell a specified amount of a given currency at a stated rate at or by a specified date in the future.

currency warrant
A warrant giving the holder the right to purchase a currency.

current delivery
Delivery of a commodity futures contract that takes place during the month the contract expires.

current delivery (month)
The futures contract which matures and becomes deliverable during the present month also called *spot month*.

current yield
The bond's annual coupon payment divided by that bond's current market price.

curvature
See **gamma**.

customer margin
Within the futures industry, financial guarantees required of both buyers and sellers of futures contracts and sellers and sometimes buyers of options contracts to ensure fulfilment of contract obligations. Margins are determined on the basis of market risk and contract value. Also referred to as *performance-bond margin*. *See* **clearing margin**.

customer's man (US)
An employee of a commission house, also called an *associated person*, broker, account executive, solicitor or registered commodity representative, who solicits or accepts and handles orders for the purchase or sale of futures or options.

custom smelter
An organization refining into bar, slab or ingot from materials (e.g., blister copper, scrap, concentrates, etc.) provided by others who then take back the refined shapes. Custom smelters derives their profit from the 'returning charge' on these activities.

cylinder
The purchase of a call and writing of a lower exercise put, or purchase of a put and writing of a lower exercise call, thereby offsetting premium cost against premium income to reduce the net payment, sometimes to zero cost. Cylinders are perhaps more usually constructed using the underlying asset as well. *See* **bull cylinder** and **bear cylinder**.

D

daily summary
A summary of contract volume, price range, open interest and settlemen prices issued by an exchange for business transacted on a daily basis.

daily trading limit
The maximum price range set by an exchange each day for a contract.

daisy chain
A term, analogous with *allocation chain*, but which pertains specifically to the chain of title to contract in dealings in physical crude oil.

Dark Northern Spring
A type of high protein hard wheat. Also known as *Hard Red Spring*.

day order/trading
An order valid throughout trading hours during day on which it is placed.

day trading
Establishing and liquidating the same position or positions within one day's trading.

day traders
Speculators who take positions in futures or options contracts and liquidate them prior to the close of the same trading day, thereby avoiding overnight margin calls.

DAX
Deutsche Aktienindex. The German stock index on 30 blue-chip equities. A future on the index is available on the Deutsche Terminborse.

dead spread
The spread obtained from selling pork belly futures and buying live hog futures, that is, to act like a slaughterhouse. The contracts are available on the Chicago Mercantile Exchange.

dealer option
A put or call on a physical commodity, not originating on or subject to the

rules of an exchange, in which the obligation for performance rests with the writer of the option.

dealing statement
A formal statement of account issued periodically by brokers to their clients covering the profit and loss and dealing charges for a specific period of time.

debit box
See **option boxes**.

debt warrant
Warrant enabling the holder to buy a bond or debt at a fixed price over a given period of time.

deck
The orders a floor broker holds in his or her hand.

dedicated line
A telephone circuit closed to public access.

default[1]
Failure to perform on a futures contract as required by exchange rules, such as failure to meet a margin call or to make or to take delivery.

default[2]
The theoretical eventuality of a contract failure.

deferred (delivery) month
The more distant month(s) in which futures trading is taking place, as distinguished from the nearby (delivery) month.

deferred futures
The futures, of those currently traded, that expire during the most distant months; also called *forward months*.

deferred pay-out option
An American option where settlement is at expiry.

deferred-start option
An option purchased before its life commences. This might be used by investors who want to lock into current pricing for options they knows they will need in the future.

deferred strike option
An option, usually on foreign exchange, where the exercise or strike price is established at a future date from a prescribed formula based on the spot exchange rate on that future date.

deliverable grades
The standard grades of commodities or instruments listed in the rules of the exchanges that must be met when delivering cash commodities against futures contracts. Grades are often accompanied by a schedule of discounts and premiums allowable for delivery of commodities of lesser or greater quality than the standard called for by the exchange. Also referred to as *contract grades*.

deliverable stocks
Commodities located in exchange-approved storage which may be used in making delivery on futures contracts.

delivery
The settlement of a futures contract by the transfer of the financial instrument or cash commodity from the seller of a futures contract to the buyer of a futures contract. Each futures exchange has specific procedures for delivery of a cash commodity. Some futures contracts, such as stock index contracts, are cash settled. There are three types of delivery: *current* - delivery during the present month; *nearby* delivery during the nearest active month; *distant* - delivery in a month further off.

delivery date
Date on which the underlying financial instrument or commodity must be delivered to fulfil the terms of the contract.

delivery instrument
A document used to effect delivery on a commodity futures contract, such as a warehouse receipt or shipping certificate.

delivery month
The specified month within which a futures contract matures and can be settled by delivery.

delivery notice
The written notice given by sellers of their intention to make delivery against open short futures positions on a particular date. This notice, delivered through the clearing house, is separate and distinct from the warehouse receipt or other instrument that will be used to transfer title.

delivery point
A specific geographic area, usually a port, within which warehouses may be listed and approved by an exchange for the issue of warehouse warrants. Many factors, geographical, economic etc., may determine the choice of a delivery point, which thereafter become a matter of exchange policy. Delivery points are locations designated by futures exchanges to which the commodity may be physically delivered.

delivery price
Price fixed by clearing house at which futures deliveries are invoiced. Also price at which a commodities futures contract is settled when deliveries are made. Also known as *invoice price*.

delta
A measure of how much an option premium changes, given a unit change in the underlying futures or cash price. Delta often is interpreted as the probability that the option will move in-the-money by expiration. The delta also measures the neutral hedge ratio, and the number of underlying contracts an option holder is long or short. The delta is derived from option pricing models and the volatility assumptions input to these on which it is dependent. Change the volatility and the delta changes. *See also* **implied delta, charm**.

delta hedge
The process of hedging with options to ensure that movements in the value of the underlying asset are exactly offset by movements in the value of a contrary options position. The delta is the ratio of change in options price for a change in asset price. If the delta is 0.25 then, if the asset moves 10 points, the option will move 2½ points. Thus, four options are needed for each unit of the asset for the movement value to be the same. If one holds the asset and fears a price fall, then it is desirable to hold an options position that will rise if the asset falls. Therefore, sell calls or buy puts in the ratio of ⅛ for each contract value of the asset held. If hedging a purchase then buy calls or sell puts. Note that this is a dynamic strategy. The delta measure is only good for small changes in the asset price and, as the asset moves in price, the delta will change and the number of contracts may need adjusting. A gamma neutral position will reduce this. Also the delta is altered by changes in the volatility (*vega*), time to expiry (*theta*), and interest rates (*rho*). Rebalancing may be required for all these reasons.

delta neutral
A position is said to be delta neutral if it has a delta of zero. Such a position

will not change in value if the underlying moves, so long as the move in the underlying asset is small. *See* **delta hedge**.

DEM
Standard foreign exchange code for Deutschemark(s).

dematerialization
The concept of moving, particularly in the securities markets, towards a system of paperless transactions and electronic share certification and registration.

deposit
Sum of money required by brokers from their clients, usually ten per cent of the value of the contract, to justify opening of a futures position.

depository or warehouse receipt
A document issued by a bank, warehouse or other depository indicating ownership of a stored commodity. In the case of many commodities deliverable against futures contracts, transfer of ownership of an appropriate depository receipt may effect contract delivery.

derivatives
Instruments derived from securities or physical markets, essentially futures and options. Thus options on equities or futures on grain are derived from the underlying cash markets and hence may be termed derivatives.

descending triangle
A chart pattern that signals a continuation of a downtrend.

designated broker
Firms committed to offer a comprehensive broking and execution service in a specific contract.

Designated Investment Exchange
An overseas investment exchange not carrying on a market in the UK may seek this status so that UK firms using it avoid onerous reporting requirements they would otherwise have to fulfil to SIB. DIEs include ISMA, CBOT, CBOE, CME, PHLX and many others.

designated market-maker
A person or firm who undertakes to make continuous offers and bids at a minimum price fluctuation level and for minimum size in a specific contract.

details (foreign exchange and currency deposit markets)
Information a dealer requires after the completion of a transaction, i.e., name, rate and dates.

Deutsche Terminbörse (DTB)
Located in Frankfurt, it lists contracts on the DAX, Bunds and individual stock options.

devaluation
A formal 'official' decrease in the exchange rate for a currency. For example, when the pound was devalued in 1967, the exchange rate, or price in terms of US dollars, went from $2.80/pound to $2.40/pound.

Dfl
Textual abbreviation for Netherlands guilder(s).

diagonal spread (options)
A combination of a vertical spread strategy placed over different expiry months. This combines a vertical and horizontal (calendar or time spread).

diagonal straddle calendar spread
Purchase of a near month straddle combined with the sale of a far month straddle at a different strike price. *See also* **straddle calendar spread**.

Dibid
Dublin interbank bid rate.

Dibor
Dublin interbank offered rate.

DIE
Designated Investment Exchange. (UK)

difference (LME)
Exchange term for the difference between an opening and closing price of a contract or opening and delivery. The net payment of variation margin.

difference option
An option whose payout is the difference between two underlying assets. The exercise price is defined in terms of the initial reference point for valuing the option. Such an option would allow trading on inter-market spreads such as TED, BED, NOB or JGBs against Bunds etc. It might also be on the

spread between US dollar and Deutschemark three-month offered rates at a certain number of basis points.

differential
When quoting a spread transaction in derivatives, the difference in price between the delivery months involved in the trade as opposed to the outright value of an individual delivery or contract month.

differentials
Premiums paid for grades better than basic grade (or *par*) or discounts allowed for grades below basic grade.

digital options
Cheaper forms of options which have a discontinuous pay out profile instead of the usual smooth profile. They pay out a fixed amount if the underlying reaches a predetermined level. The two types are all-or-nothing options and one-touch options. For an investor with a precise view of the market these options can be cheaper than conventional options because the payout is restricted and not open-ended. They can be added together to create assets that exactly mirror investors' anticipated index price movements, for example.

dirty price
The price of a bond including accrued interest.

disc
Discretionary order.

discount
The amount by which one price is below another. Also the amount a price would be reduced to purchase a commodity of lesser grade. Sometimes used to refer to the price differences between futures of different delivery months, as in the phrase 'July is at a discount to May', indicating that the prices of the July futures is lower than that of May. Applies to cash prices that are below the future. *See also* **contango** and **backwardation**.

discount basis
A method of quoting securities wherein the price is expressed as an annualized discount from maturity value. It applies especially in the money markets.

discount rate
The interest rate charged on loans by the Federal Reserve to member banks. Also the rate at which money market instruments are sold.

discount security
A security sold at a discount to its par value. This would clearly include Treasury bills and zero coupon bonds that pay no separate coupons or dividends and where all the investment return is in the form of capital gain.

discretionary account
An arrangement by which the holder of the account gives written power of attorney to another person, often his or her broker, to make trading decisions. Also known as a *controlled* or *managed account*.

discretionary order
This is a limit order which allows the broker to buy at a higher price or sell at a lower price within an agreed boundary of discretion granted by the client.

distant delivery month
Delivery of a commodity in a further month.

distant months
The far-dated delivery (or exercise) months in a futures (or options) contract.

dividend
That part of a company s post tax profits distributed to shareholders, normally expressed in pence per share. It is a discretionary payment, not a fixed amount, except in the case of preference shares. *See also* **interim dividend** and **final dividend**.

DKK
Standard foreign exchange code for Danish krone(r).

DKr
Textual abbreviation for Danish krone(r).

DM, Dm
Textual abbreviations for Deutschemark(s).

DMI
Direct Member Input, i.e. a member can enter his/her own trades into the trade registration system of the exchange. Used in connection with TRS.

double barrier option
An option which is both capped and extinguishable. An option that has two in-strikes, out-strikes, or trigger prices. These were offered first by Westminster Equity. *See* **barrier option**.

double 'O'
A colloquialism meaning, in terms of contract price, the whole number. For example, an interest rate contract that moves from a price of 93.99 to 94.01 will have passes through the 'double o' of 94.00.

double option
An option which gives the buyer or person taking the option the right either to buy from or sell to the writer of the option or the person who gives it the underlying instrument at the strike price. Essentially it is an option that can be exercised either as a call or as a put. Such options are available on the London Stock Exchange (its conventional or traditional options) and on the LME.

double top (double bottom)
A chart reversal pattern. It is two peaks (troughs) breaking a trendline. The average height of the peaks (troughs) shows the minimum likely price move out of the pattern.

down-and-in option
See **barrier option**.

down-and-out option
See **barrier option**.

DSR
Delivery Status Report.

DTI
Department of Trade and Industry. (UK)

DTB
See **Deutsche Terminbörse**.

dual-currency bond
A bond where the coupon interest is payable in one currency, but it is redeemed in another currency.

dual-currency option
An option that allows the holder to buy either of two currencies.

dual-strike option
An interest rate option, usually either a cap or floor, with one rate for part of the option's life and another for the rest of its life. Essentially it is two options running back to back, one being a deferred-start option.

dumping
Selling goods in foreign markets at cost price or below to gain market share or to reduce over supply.

DVP
Delivery versus payment.

E

earlies[1]
Up to and including the 15th of the month in respect of euronotes and CDs.

earlies[2]
Early, as distinct from main, crop potatoes. Before the skins have set.

econometrics
The application of statistical and mathematical methods in the field of economics to test and quantify economic theories and the solutions to economic problems.

ECU
Standard foreign exchange code for the European currency unit (Ecu).

Ecu
European currency unit, the accounting unit of the European Community in which bonds and other government and corporate issues, derivatives contracts etc. are made. Its composition is based on a basket of currencies in the European exchange rate mechanism and may change from time to time.

EDS
Enter day stop order.

EDSP
Exchange delivery settlement price, the price at which futures contracts are settled for delivery, the balance being paid over by way of margin to achieve the price of the contract.

EEP
Exports Enhancement Programme, 1985. (US)

EFP
See **exchange for physicals**.

EFS
Exchange of futures for swaps. *See* **exchange for physicals**.

elasticity
A characteristic of commodities that describes the interaction of the supply and demand and the price of a commodity.

elbow trade
A colloquialism meaning a trade executed very quietly and with a person quite close or adjacent to another in a trading crowd. Such a trade may be ruled invalid, as it is contrary to the fair meaning and interpretation of 'open outcry'.

embedded options
Options, usually interest rate options, embedded in debt instruments or bonds that affect its redemption date. These include put and call features on bonds, and also include mortgage-backed securities. Dual-dated gilts would also qualify.

end/end (foreign exchange and currency deposit markets)
Forward swaps or currency deposits arranged for implementation before or at spot delivery on the last working day of the month should be described as 'end/end' if it is intended that they should mature on the last working day of the appropriate future month.

enter day stop order
This type of order instructs the broker to put a stop order at a particular price on a previous trade. This type of order is cancelled automatically at the end of the trading day.

enter open stop
This order is the same as an EDS but remains on the broker's books until executed or cancelled.

entry price
The price at which a derivatives contract position is opened.

EOE
See **European Options Exchange**.

EOS
Enter open stop order.

equilibrium price
The market price at which the quantity supplied of a commodity equals the quantity demanded.

equity[1]
Common stock or shares.

equity[2]
The residual value of a futures trading account assuming it was liquidated at current prices.

equity convertible
A bond, usually an unsecured loan stock, which is convertible into the equity of the issuing company.

equity LEAPS
See **LEAPS**.

equity warrant
A warrant, usually attached to a bond but capable of being separated and/or trading separately, entitling the holder to purchase shares. The shares are usually those of the warrant issuing company but not always.

ERA
See **exchange rate agreement**.

erratic
A market that moves rapidly, changes direction quickly and is irregular in its action.

ESP
Standard foreign exchange code for Spanish peseta(s).

ETO
Exchange traded option.

Euroclear
An international clearing system for settling transactions in securities, but especially eurobonds and eurosecurities. Owned by over 100 banks, it is provided under contract by Morgan Guaranty and is based in Brussels.

euro-commercial paper
A generic term applied to the market for euronotes issued on a non-underwritten basis. Euro-commercial paper is commonly issued on a continuous tap basis by one or more dealers. *See* **eurosecurity**.

eurodollars
US dollars on deposit with a bank outside of the US and, consequently, outside the jurisdiction of the US. The bank could be either a foreign bank or a subsidiary of a US bank.

euronote
A short-term fully-negotiable bearer promissory note typically of up to six months maturity. Euronotes are commonly distributed by an auction between members of a tender panel. *See* **eurosecurity**.

EOE
See **European Options Exchange**.

European option
An option that can be exercised only on the expiry date.

European Options Exchange (EOE-Optibeurs)
Located in Amsterdam, it lists contracts on stock indices, bonds and currencies.

eurosecurity
A security denominated in a currency other than that of the market in which it is issued, e.g., a dollar-denominated bond issued in the UK or Germany.

evening up
Buying or selling to offset an existing market position.

ex
Opposite of **cum**. A share bought ex-dividend, ex-rights or ex-capitalization will not entitle the purchaser to obtain the next dividend, or rights issue etc. This is because it takes time for company registrars to update share owner records. Hence there will be an ex-dividend date after which the share will change hands without there being time to update ownership records. The new owner will not obtain the dividend and will pay a lower price in recognition of this.

excess
The amount by which the equity exceeds the original margin requirements in a trader's futures account.

exchange fee
A fixed fee levied by an exchange on its members in respect of all business

transacted. Exchange fees will normally be an exchange's main source of revenue.

exchange for physicals (EFP)/exchange of futures for swaps (EFS)
A transaction generally used by two hedgers who want to exchange futures for cash positions. It is the exchange of a futures position for a physical position (swap position). This swap of cash for futures takes place through the exchange. Also referred to as *against actuals (AA)* or *versus cash*.

exchange rate agreement
A synthetic agreement for forward exchange developed by Barclays Bank. In contrast to a forward exchange agreement it is settled without reference to the spot rate and does not reflect changes in the spot market.

exchange rate futures
Futures contracts for currencies.

execution
The fulfilling of an order to buy or sell by a member trading an exchange contract at or as near as possible to any price stated in the order. Both the price made, and time of the trade must be recorded.

exercise
To 'exercise an option' is to use the right to buy or sell the underlying asset at the strike price.

exercise notice
A notice in writing delivered to a clearing house on or by a specific time giving notice of intent from an option holder (buyer) that they wish to make or take delivery of the underlying instrument or commodity.

exercise price
Same as **strike price**.

exhaustion gap
A price pattern that is a gap appearing near the end of a trend. A filling of the gap by a move back through it indicates a trend reversal.

exit price
The price at which a derivatives contract position is closed out. The difference between the exit and entry prices reflects the profit/loss.

expanded trading hours
Additional trading hours of specific futures and options contracts that overlap with business hours in other time zones.

expiration
The end of an option's life.

expiration date
The last day that an option may be exercised into the underlying asset or future. Options on futures can expire on the last trading day of the future or on a specific date during the month preceding the futures contract delivery month. For example, for the latter, an option on a March futures contract expires in February but is referred to as a March option because its exercise would result in a March futures contract position.

ex-pit transaction
Trades executed, for certain technical purposes, in a location other than the regular exchange trading pit or ring.

Export Enhancement Programme, 1985 (US)
Introduced in May 1985 with the declared intention of regaining for the US markets that it considered lost to countries indulging in unfair trade practices. It offered traders subsidies or bonuses in the form of commodities held in government stocks. It applied to wheat and barley.

extendible
A feature that gives an investor the right to extend the investment on the same terms.

extinguishable option
An option where the holder's right to exercise is cancelled if the value of the underlying passes a specified level. See **barrier option**.

extrinsic value
That part of the premium of an option which is not intrinsic value. See **time value**.

F

face value
The amount of money printed on the face of the certificate of a security; the original amount of indebtedness incurred.

fail (actual default)
A contract failure is the actual, as opposed to the theoretical, default by one or both parties to a transaction.

fair futures price
The theoretical price of a future calculated such that there is no cash and carry arbitrage opportunity.

FAS
Free Alongside Ship. Delivered free on the dock or wharf.

FAST
Fast Automated Screen Trading. This is the London Commodity Exchange's screen trading system. It automatically matches bids and offers on a computer screen.

fast market
A state or condition of a market wherein trading volatility is such that only transaction levels or significant price movements can faithfully be reported. During such times no attempt by an exchange to cover price quotations will be made, and brokers who have accepted orders from clients to be executed at specific levels will not normally be held to those levels.

FAZ
Frankfurter Allgemeine Zeitung German stock index of 100 stocks.

FCOJ
Frozen concentrated orange juice.

Federal Funds[1]
Member bank deposits held by the Federal Reserve; these funds are loaned by the Federal Reserve to other member banks.

Federal funds[2]
The wire transfer service for payments.

Federal funds rate
The rate of interest charged for the use of federal funds.

Federal Housing Administration (FHA)
A division of the US Department of Housing and Urban Development that insures residential mortgage loans and sets construction standards.

Federal Reserve System
A central banking system in the US, created by the Federal Reserve Act in 1913, designed to assist the nation in attaining its economic and financial goals. The structure of the Federal Reserve System includes a Board of Governors, the Federal Open Market Committee, and 12 Federal Reserve Banks. The 'Fed.' has the responsibility for implementing monetary policy and regulating the national banking structure.

feed ratio
A ratio used to express the relationship of feeding costs to the dollar value of livestock. *See* **hog/corn ratio** and **steer/corn ratio**.

FFr
Textual abbreviation for French franc(s).

fictitious trading
Wash trading, bucketing, cross trading, or other device, scheme or artifice to give the appearance of trading where no competitive trade has occurred.

FIEX-35
A Spanish capital weighted index of the 35 most liquid equities, formerly listed on Mofex.

fill
The complete execution of an order.

fill-or-kill order (FOK)
A customer order that is a price limit order that must be filled immediately on price or size or cancelled.

FIM
Standard foreign exchange code for Finnish markka.

FIMBRA
Financial Intermediaries Managers and Brokers Regulatory Authority. (UK)

final dividend
The dividend a company pays at the end of its financial year, as recommended by the directors but authorized by the shareholders at the company's Annual General Meeting (AGM). *See also* **dividend** and **interim dividend**.

Financial Analysis Auditing Compliance Tracking System (FACTS)
The National Futures Association's computerized system of maintaining financial records of its member firms and monitoring their financial conditions. (US)

financial instruments
Currency, securities, and indices of their value. Examples include shares, mortgages, commercial paper and Treasury bills and bonds.

Financiële Termijnmarkt Amsterdam (FTA)
A Dutch exchange which lists futures contracts on Dutch bonds, stock indices, and the US dollar.

FINEX
A division of the New York Cotton Exchange, FINEX lists US Treasury note, dollar index and Ecu futures.

Finnish Options Market (FOM)
Located in Helsinki, it lists contracts on currencies, interest rates and stock indices.

firm (sterling deposits)
When principals put brokers on 'firm' and no specific amount is mentioned, the principals are bound to deal in a marketable amount at the quoted price provided that the names are acceptable. When brokers quote without qualification they are bound to deal firm in a marketable amount at the time they make the quote, provided that the names are acceptable. (*Bank of England Grey Book*).

firm (foreign exchange and currency deposit markets)
Dealers making an offer or bid on a 'firm' basis commit principals but they would be advised to add some qualification (e.g. 'firm for one minute' or 'firm for one million only').

first month
The shortest maturity contract still trading. *See also* front month, spot month.

first notice day
The first day on which notices are issued by sellers to the clearing house, and by the clearing house to a buyer indicating delivery in a specific delivery month.

flag
A chart continuation pattern lasting one to three weeks.

fix (price fix)
Conventionally, the use of a derivatives contract price at a specific time used to fix the price of a physical commodity for delivery, shipping or insurance purposes.

fixed-to-fixed convertible
A fixed-rate bond that is convertible into another fixed-rate bond.

fixed trade
An illegal transaction fixed in the sense that it was subject to prior arrangement and not executed competitively.

fiva
Forward or futures contract on implied volatility.

floating-rate note
A bond that pays a coupon that is set off a reference rate, e.g. Libor + x%. In other words, it does not carry a fixed rate of interest.

floor
A series of European exercise interest rate call options contracts whereby the seller will refund to a holder the difference between current interest rates and an agreed strike rate should rates fall below the floor. They thus provide a hedge for investors or companies wanting to provide a certain return on floating-rate assets, and are thus effectively a string of interest rate guarantees. Like caps, with which they may be combined to form collars, they are based on a reference rate such as three-month or six-month Libor. Sellers will be persons expecting rates to rise. Opposite of a **cap**.

floor broker
A person who buys or sells futures contracts for others on the exchange trading floor.

floor committee
A delegation of senior exchange floor members who are generally responsible for recommendation of additions and alterations to the trading rules, enforcement of the trading rules, rulings on trading disputes and consideration of applicants for trading rights.

floor member
A corporate member of an exchange. Holders of this membership may transact business for themselves and on behalf of clients. They generally hold voting shares in the exchange.

floor price display board
A price display system used on market floors to reflect all current trading information.

floortion
An option on a floor. For the holder, this is an option to buy a floor at a predetermined rate and date. Floortions may be used by an investment body that needs to guarantee a certain level of return, but is unsure of the exact level of funding it will receive. It may buy some floors for the funds it is sure it will get and floortions for an extra unknown amount. *See also* **compound options, caption**.

floor trader
An exchange member or employee who executes trades by being personally present in the pit or place for futures or options trading.

FM
Textual abbreviation for Finnish markka.

f.o.b
Free on board. A contractual term indicating that the price quoted to the buyer is the price of goods plus the cost of putting them on board the vessel which will carry them. Freight and insurance must then be paid by the buyer.

FOFs
Futures and options funds.

FOK
Fill or kill order.

FOM
See **Finnish Options Market**.

Footsie
Colloquial term for the FT-SE 100 share index.

f.o.r
As for f.o.b, but meaning 'free on rail'. Price quote includes cost of transport to rail head or station, from which goods will be sent.

for
The key preposition in a trader's quotation signifying an order for purchase, e.g. "ten for thirty (lots of) Dec(ember)". *See also* **at**.

forecast volatility
Estimates of future volatility. *See* **volatility**.

foreign exchange
Foreign currency. On the foreign exchange market, foreign currency is bought and sold for immediate or forward delivery.

forex
Foreign exchange.

forward
See **forward contract**.

forward band
A zero-cost collar, i.e. one in which the premium paid for the cap is offset by the premium gained from selling the floor.

forward break
Citibank's name for a **break-forward**.

forward contract
A contract in which a seller agrees to deliver to a buyer sometime in the future. Forward contracts, in contrast to futures contracts, are privately negotiated and are not exchange traded or standardized. There is no margin paid over between the counterparties, only a settlement on the agreed date.

forward exchange agreement (FXA)
A synthetic agreement for forward exchange (SAFE) developed by Midland Montagu. In contrast to a forward exchange rate agreement, it is settled based on the difference between the spot rate and the forward rate.

forward (foreign exchange and currency deposit markets)
All deals over two working days from today for periods of one month onward fixed at the time of dealing. (All deals for a broken number of days up to the one month date are known as *shorts* or *short dates*). Where the maturity falls on a non-trading day, it takes place on the following working day. Where the deal is arranged on a day for which spot delivery occurs on the last working day of the month, it matures on the last working day of the appropriate month in the future. Where deals are trading for, say, 3 months forward, the maturity date will be taken as 3 months from the spot settlement date. If this maturity date falls on either a weekend or a bank holiday the maturity date will be on the next business day unless that day is in the following month in which case it should be the day prior to the bank holiday or weekend.

forward-forward (foreign exchange and currency deposit markets)
A forward sale against a forward purchase or forward purchase against a forward sale. It involves the short-term exchange of currency deposits.

forward-forward deposit
An agreement by one party to make a deposit with another at a specified future date and rate.

forward market
Refers to informal (non-exchange) trading of commodities or other assets to be delivered at a future date. Contracts for forward delivery are 'personalized' i.e., delivery time and amount are as determined between each seller and customer. *See* **forward contract**.

forward months
Futures contracts, of those currently traded, calling for later or distant delivery. Also described as *deferred contracts*.

forward purchase or sale
A purchase or sale of an actual commodity for deferred delivery.

forward rate agreement (FRA)
A contract to provide a given interest rate, for a given maturity, from a date in the future. FRAs are both purchased and sold. Quotations are made on

the basis of bid and offer yield levels for the period of the FRA. They are labelled on the basis of the number of months to the start and end of the FRA. For example, a three-month FRA starting one month forward, would be termed a 1x4 FRA. It starts in one month and ends after four. There is no transfer of cash until the date at which the FRA will commence, when a single payment is made to offset the difference between current rates and the strike rate of the FRA. It is thus a contract for a difference. FRAs are more flexible than short-term interest rate futures to the extent that they allow forward rates to be fixed to cover periods not normally covered by futures contracts. The disadvantage is that, like other forward agreements, contracts are not of a standard (or fungible) nature and, unlike futures, there is no clearing house to cover the risk introduced by the presence of the counterparty. FRAs offer opportunities for risk management, cashflow matching, and forward rate speculation. An FRA can clearly be used to manage interest rate risk by locking-in a known forward rate. Hence, an institution with a fixed liability at some future date can immunize itself from interest rate risk through the use of an FRA. Following on from this, FRAs provide an ideal instrument for matching asset and liability cash flows exactly, for FRAs can be tailored to suit the exact dates required. FRAs can be used speculatively by locking-in a forward funding or investment rate in the expectation that rates will not achieve the levels implied by the market. FRAs are off-balance sheet, with no margin payments, and the credit risk is limited to the difference between the contracted rate and the prevailing rate.

forward rate bracket
Terminology used by First National Bank of Chicago for a **range forward**.

forward spread agreement
A contract designed by the Hongkong and Shanghai Banking Corporation. The counterparties contract into a spread between two forward rate agreement (FRA) rates applied to a nominal amount of one currency. The settlement amount is the spread between prevailing Libor plus or minus the contracted spread.

forward start option
An option that provides the purchaser the right, after a contracted period of time, to hold a standard put or call option with an at-the-money exercise price at the time the option is granted rather than when it is activated.

FOX
See **London Fox**.

FRA
Forward rate agreement.

FRAption or fraption
An option on an FRA. Also known as an *interest rate guarantee*.

free supply
Stocks of a commodity which are available for commercial sale, as distinguished from government-owned or controlled stocks.

freight forward
Term indicating the freight on goods is payable at the port of destination.

FRF
Standard foreign exchange code for French franc(s).

FRN
Floating-rate note.

front month
The shortest maturity contract month trading. *See also* **first month** or **spot month**.

front running
The illegal practice of trading ahead of a client's orders.

front spread
A ratio spread. *See* **call** or **put ratio spreads**.

FSA[1]
The Financial Services Act 1986, as amended from time to time.

FSA[2]
Forward spread agreement.

FTA
See **Financiële Termijnmarket Amsterdam**.

FTSE-100 Index
Index of 100 major **UK** shares listed on the London Stock Exchange. It was drawn up specifically to be used for a futures contract and trades on LIFFE as a future and as a European- and American-style option.

fugit
The probability of early exercise on an American-style option. It is measured either in per cent, or on a comparable scale of zero to ten. It is a product of the delta and the theta. In practice, it is little used.

full carrying charge market
A futures market where the price difference between delivery months reflects the total costs of interest, insurance and storage.

full membership
A membership that allows the holder to trade all futures and options contracts listed by the exchange.

fundamental analysis
A method of anticipating future price movement using supply and demand information. *Not* technical analysis.

fungibility
The characteristic of inter-changeabiltity. Futures contracts for the same commodity and delivery month are fungible due to their standardized specifications for quality, delivery date and delivery locations. A second tranche of government bond issues if identical to an earlier issue can become fungible with it, making it one single bond issue as far as investors are concerned.

FUTOP
See **Copenhagen Stock Exchange & Guarantee Fund for Danish Options and Futures**.

future rate agreement
A forward rate agreement, FRA.

futures
A term used to designate all contracts covering the purchase and sale of physical commodities or financial instruments for future delivery on a commodity exchange. *See* **futures contract**.

futures at discount to cash
A backwardation in the market. Futures prices are lower than the current market price.

futures at premium to cash
A contango or carrying charge market where futures prices are higher than the current market price.

futures commission merchant (FCM)
An individual or organization that solicits or accepts orders to buy or sell futures contracts, options or options on futures and accepts money or other assets from customers to support such orders. Also referred to as *commission house* or *wire house*.

futures contract
A legally binding agreement, usually made on a futures exchange, to buy or sell a commodity or financial instrument sometime in the future. Futures contracts are standardized according to the quality, quantity, and delivery time and location for each commodity or financial asset. The only variable is price, which is discovered on an exchange trading floor. The exchange or clearing house guarantees performance of the contract. OTC futures are not so standardized and are essentially margined forwards.

futures-type settlement
The settlement procedure used on exchanges where the purchase of the contract requires no initial cash outlay. Cash settlement is made each day based on the difference between the current day's closing price and the previous day's closing price or the original trade price.

future volatility
What volatility will be in the future. Can only be forecast or estimated and is unknown. See **volatility**.

FX
Foreign exchange.

FXA
See **forward exchange agreement**.

G

G-10
The ten lending industrial nations of the world. Specifically, the United States, Canada, England, Belgium, France, Germany, Italy, The Netherlands, Sweden and Japan. Also variously exists as G-5 and G-7.

gamma
A measurement of how fast delta changes, given a unit change in the underlying futures price. It is positive for long options positions and negative for short options positions. It is always greatest for at-the-money options and decreases as the price of the underlying asset moves away from the exercise price. Gamma is greater for short-term options than for longer maturity options. If a positive price change in the underlying leads to an increase in an option's delta (and a negative move reduces it), the position is said to have positive gamma. All spreads that are helped by movement in the underlying market have a positive gamma. It is advantageous for a position to have positive gamma. A rise in prices will increase the delta of the option and the position may be re-hedged by selling the underlying at a higher price. Conversely, a price fall will reduce the delta and the position may be re-hedged by buying the underlying at a lower price. In both cases the position has generated a profit. Generally, positions with positive gamma are those that are long of options and have positive vega and theta. *See also* **colour** and **speed**.

gaps
Price patterns on charts where the highest (lowest) price of one day is followed by the lowest (highest) price of the next day being significantly higher (lower) leaving a gap in the chart. *See* **breakaway gap, runaway gap, measuring gap** and **exhaustion gap**.

Garman Kohlhagen option pricing model
A model for evaluating European options on foreign currencies.

GBP
Standard foreign exchange code for British pound(s).

GD
Good for the day, an order type.

gearing[1]
The ability to gain exposure to a larger monetary value of an asset, financial instrument or commodity with a comparatively small amount of capital. Futures and options, where margin or premium form the initial down payment, offer high gearing. *See also* **leverage**.

gearing[2]
A company's debt (bank debt, bond issues etc.) as a percentage of its equity capital. High gearing means a high level of debt in relation to capital.

GEMMs
Gilt-edged market-makers. The market-makers in UK government debt. They are required to make markets in all gilt issues, expected to bid for new stock, and subject to supervision by the Bank of England, Stock Exchange and SFA.

GEMx
The German Equity Market index that provides a contract for OMLX London. It comprises 20 shares traded in London and Germany. The index is provided for OMLX by Dextel Findata AB.

GFOFs
Geared futures and options funds. (UK)

G-hedge
A form of range forward offered by Generale Bank that differs from the usual style in having a fixed commission and a symmetrical range around the forward rate.

gilt
Gilt-edged stock or UK government debt. Many varieties of such bonds are available of all maturities including straights, dual-dated, convertible, index-linked, floating-rate and undated and Ecu-denominated (although, technically, the Ecu issues are not classified as gilts). Virtually all pay coupons semi-annually, although the Ecus pay annually.

Ginnie Mae
See **GNMA**.

give-up[1]
At the request of the customer, a brokerage house which has not performed the service is credited with the execution of an order.

give-up[2]
To allocate title to an executed transaction to a third party. In the trading pit, a broker 'gives up' the name of the firm for which he or she was acting to another member with whom a transaction has just been completed. Give-ups in the pit are not allowed, brokers deal with each other in the pit as principal to principal and all trades must be processed in the name of the executing broker, thus give-ups can only be effected through the formal process of allocation.

give-up[3]
The loss of yield, resulting from the sale of securities at one yield and purchase of securities at a lower yield. *See* **pick-up**.

GLOBEX
Global Electronic Exchange jointly developed by the CME, CBOT, Reuters and MATIF. It is an electronic trading system which displays prices of various contracts around the world. Bids and offers are shown, together with market size. Deals can be done on screen and confirmation is shown almost instantaneously. It is not currently a 24-hour system.

GNMA
Pass-through mortgage-backed certificates guaranteed by the US Government National Mortgage Association (GNMA or Ginnie Mae). The certificates are backed by pools of Federal Housing Association (FHA) insured and/or Veteran's Administration (VA) guaranteed residential mortgages, with the mortgage and note held in safekeeping by a custodial financial institution.

gold swap
Sale of gold under an agreement to repurchase later.

gold warrant
A separate or attached warrant exercisable into gold at a predetermined price. They are listed and traded on some exchanges, including the American Stock Exchange and Luxembourg Stock Exchange.

good-'til-cancelled order (GTC)
Order which is valid at any time during market hours until executed or cancelled by the client. The order will specify a desired price.

Government National Mortgage Association
A division of the US Department of Housing and Urban Development; created in 1968.

grain terminal
Large grain elevator facility with the capacity to ship grain by rail and/or barge to domestic or foreign markets.

grades
Various qualities of a commodity.

grading
The process of determining the standard or quality of a commodity against the derivative contract standard and hence the delivery premium or discount of the physical commodity.

grading certificate
The certificate of quality issued by a commodity exchange against samples submitted for grading.

grantor
The maker, writer, or seller of an option contract.

Grey Book
The Bank of England's rules for 'The Regulation of the Wholesale Markets in Sterling, Foreign Exchange and Bullion' and its publication The London Code of Conduct for Principals and Broking Firms in the Wholesale Markets.

gross national product (GNP)
The total value of final goods and services produced in a country over a specific time period.

gross processing margin (GPM)
The difference between the cost of soybeans and the combined sales of income of the processed soybean oil and meal. Other industries have similar formulas to express the relationship of raw material costs to sales income from finished products.

GTC
Good-'til-cancelled order.

growths
Description of commodities such as cotton, coffee or sugar according to area in which they are is produced.

guarantee
As applied to the function of a clearing house, means that the performance of a transaction properly executed and registered on an exchange which the clearing house is contracted to, is guaranteed and therefore assured, in the event that one of the parties to the original transaction defaults.

guts
A strangle formed from in-the-money options, i.e. buy a call and buy a put at a higher exercise price when the underlying's price lies between the two exercise prices.

H

haircut
The discount applied by the clearing house to assets such as government bonds deposited as margin collateral. On US option exchanges, the money deposited by traders with the clearing house to ensure the integrity of their positions. It is similar to **margin**.

hand signals
Signals used by traders on the floor of an exchange to supplement spoken bids and offers.

Hang Seng Index
The Hong Kong equity index on about 30 stocks representing 70% of market turnover.

Hard Red Spring
A type of high protein wheat. Also known as *Dark Northern Spring*.

Hard Red Winter
A type of high protein hard wheat.

head and shoulders
A major chart reversal pattern. It is formed of a left shoulder peak (trough), a head as a higher peak (lower trough), and a right shoulder peak (trough). It may thus be a top or bottom pattern. A neckline may be drawn which is used to indicate the minimum reversal move. A failed head and shoulder acts as a continuation pattern.

Heath-Jarrow-Morton option pricing model
A model for pricing interest rate options. It takes an exogenous approach to the initial yield curve and is a multi-factor model.

heating oil
Synonymous to No 2 fuel oil, a distillate fuel oil for domestic heating use.

heavy
A market in which current prices are demonstrating a tendency to decline.

heavy oil
Opposite of light oil.

hedge
Protecting the price of a financial instrument or commodity at a date in the future by undertaking an offsetting position using futures, options or another instrument. If the move in the cash market is adverse to the needs of the investor, producer or consumer, then opposite moves in the derivatives market position will eliminate or reduce the risk and loss. *See also* **hedger**.

hedger
An individual or company owning, or planning to own, a cash commodity— corn, soybeans, wheat, US Treasury bonds, notes, bills, etc.—and concerned that the cost of the commodity may change before either buying (or selling) it in the cash market. A hedger achieves protection against changing cash prices by purchasing (selling) futures contracts of the same or similar commodity and later offsetting that position by selling (purchasing) futures contracts of the same quantity and type as the initial transaction or undergoing delivery if the hedge date is the delivery date. Similar methods can be deployed with options positions. If an asset is held and a price fall is feared, then put options may be purchased. If it is intended to purchase the asset or commodity then a call option may be bought. Better protection is usually obtained here by selling the options back, thus realizing time value, rather than exercising them. *See also* **delta hedge**.

hedge ratio (futures)
The number of contracts required to hedge one contract's value of the underlying asset. This is not always one contract. For example, to hedge the cheapest to deliver bond use nominal value of position/nominal value of contract multiplied by the price factor of the cheapest to deliver to obtain the required number of contracts. Close position on hedge date or at expiry.

hedge ratio (options)
The delta of an option derived from an option valuation model. It tells the proportion of options and underlying assets that will create a theoretically riskless hedge. *See also* **delta hedge**.

Hedonic index
An index which allows for changes in the mix of the sample to isolate pure price changes.

held order
An order specific to price and which, in the event of a market trading

through the specified level, the client originating the order shall have right of claim to that price at the possible consequential loss to the broker.

held market
A market on which all client orders are deemed to be placed in the terms of a held order.

HFO
Heavy fuel oil.

Hibid
Hong Kong interbank bid rate.

Hibor
Hong Kong interbank offered rate.

high
The highest price of the day for a particular contract. In the UK, high and low prices are actual transaction highs and lows for the day. In the USA, highs and lows are frequently published as the highest significant bid and the lowest significant offer—they do not necessarily need to be actual traded levels.

hi-low option
A combination of two look-back or path-dependent options. Such an option pays the difference between the high and low during a specified period of an underlying asset, say a stock index or a stock. A purchaser would be taking a view that the volatility of the market would be higher than the implied volatility of the options in the structure. If the difference between the high and low levels is greater than the premium, the holder makes profits.

historical volatility
The measure of volatility derived from historical data. *See* **volatility**.

hit the bid
Expression meaning to sell at a bid price.

HKD
Standard foreign exchange code for Hong Kong dollar(s).

HKFE
See **Hong Kong Futures Exchange**.

hockey stick diagrams
Disparaging term for profit and loss diagrams of options positions.

hog/corn ratio
The relationship of feeding costs to the dollar value of hogs. It is measured by dividing the price of hogs ($/hundredweight) by the price of corn ($/bushel). When corn prices are high relative to pork prices, fewer units of corn equal the dollar value of 100 pounds of pork. Conversely, when corn prices are low in relation to pork prices, more units of corn are required to equal the value of 100 pounds of pork. See **feed ratio**.

holder
See **option buyer**.

Ho-Lee option pricing model
An option pricing model for interest rate options that takes account of the term structure of interest rates whilst assuming that all rates along the curve fluctuate to the same degree. There is no mean reversion and all rates along the yield curve have the same standard deviation.

Hong Kong Futures Exchange
This Far East exchange lists contracts on the Hang Seng Index, gold and three-month Hibor.

horizontal spread
The sale of either a call or put option and the simultaneous purchase of the same type of option with, typically, the same strike price but with a different and longer maturity expiration month. Also referred to as a *calendar spread*, *diagonal spread*, or *time spread*. The objective of this trade is to capitalize on faster time value decay in the short position and short maturity option compared with the long position in the longer maturity option. The long position hedges risk from exercise taking place. See **time spread**.

house order
A proprietary order originated from an exchange member's own in-house account. Known also as a *principal trade*.

how many?
A trading term in commodities relating to the number of contracts for sale or purchase. Once the price was agreed the challenge of "How many?" from one party to the other committed the challenger to a minimum of 5 contracts, a returned challenge of "How many?" from the second party was a commitment to a minimum of 10 contracts etc. etc. In most open-outcry

markets this phrase is no longer permitted as volumes must be stated with quotations.

HSI
Hang Seng Index (Hong Kong) of equities.

Hull-White option pricing model
An interest rate option pricing model that refines the Ho-Lee approach in respect of fluctuations in rates along the curve. It guarantees consistency with the initial term structure and has mean reversion thus allowing longer rates to have lower volatility than short term rates. It is a one factor model.

I

IBEX 35
Index of 35 Spanish equities.

ICC
Intermarket Clearing Corporation.

ICCH
See **International Commodities Clearing House**.

IDB
An intermediary dealer broker.

IEP
Standard foreign exchange code for Irish punt(s).

IFOX
See **Irish Futures and Options Exchange**.

IMI
International Market Index, an index of international stocks, traded as a future on the American Stock Exchange.

IMM
The International Monetary Market of the Chicago Mercantile Exchange, listing currency and interest rate futures. Its standardized trading and delivery dates have been used as the basis for some OTC markets such as FRAs.

immediate or cancel (IOC) order
An order that must be filled immediately or not at all. Such orders need not be filled in their entirety.

implied delta
Delta calculated from the implied volatility of the option rather than the volatility estimate input to the option pricing model. This delta is also known as the *price delta*.

implied volatility
The value of asset price volatility that will equate the market price of an option with the fair or model value of an option.

IMRO
Investment Managers' Regulatory Organization. (UK)

Index and Option Market
A part of the Chicago Mercantile Exchange trading stock index futures and options on indices, currencies, T-bills and eurodollars.

index contract
A futures or options contract on an index such as a stock index, e.g. FTSE-100 Index or S&P 500, etc. The index future will be quoted at so much per point, for example, £25 in the case of LIFFE's FTSE-100 contract. The contract size is thus variable depending on the level of the futures quote. Contracts open at expiry are closed out with profits or losses paid over through variation margin. Index options are usually options on the cash index rather than the future. Like index futures, they too are subject to cash settlement on exercise.

Individual clearing member
Holders of such a membership class may clear their own trades and trades of their clients, but not trades for other members of the exchange.

initial margin
The amount futures or options market participants must deposit into their margin account at the time they places an order to buy or sell a futures or options contract. This must be maintained throughout the time their position is open and is returnable at delivery, exercise, expiry or closing out.

in position
See position^2.

INS
Institutional net settlements.

institutional customer
Broadly, a client with large holdings in securities who is active in financial markets for hedging such holdings or maximizing returns on positions.

inter-commodity spread
The purchase of a given delivery month of one futures market and the si

multaneous sale of the same delivery month of a different futures market. Also referred to as an *inter-market spread*.

inter-delivery spread
The purchase of one delivery month of a given commodity futures contract and simultaneous sale of another delivery month of the same commodity on the same exchange. Also known as *intra-market spread*.

interest arbitrage
The operation wherein foreign debt instruments are purchased to profit from the higher interest rate in the foreign country over the home country.

interest rate contracts
See **long-term interest rate contracts** and **short-term interest rate contracts**.

interest rate guarantee (FRAption)
An option on a forward rate agreement. Purchasers have the right, but not obligation to take an FRA at an agreed strike price or interest rate level. A strip of interest rate guarantees form a cap.

interest rate option
Option to pay, or receive, a specified rate of interest on or from a predetermined date. *See also* **short-term interest rate contracts**.

interest rate parity
The formal theory of interest rate parity holds that, under normal conditions, the forward premium or discount on one currency in terms of another is directly related to the interest rate differential between the two countries. For example, at interest rate parity, the forward rate discount (or premium) on Swiss francs in terms of dollars would equal the premium (or discount) of interest rates in Switzerland over (or under) those in the US. This theory holds only when there are unrestricted flows of international short-term capital. In reality numerous economic and legal obstacles restrict the movement, so that actual parity is rare. *See* **covered interest arbitrage**.

interim dividend
A dividend declared part way through a company's financial year that is authorized only by the directors. *See also* **dividend** and **final dividend**.

Intermarket Clearing Corporation
A subsidiary of the OCC clearing futures for the AMEX Commodities Corporation, New York Futures Exchange and the Philadelphia Board of Trade. OCC provides operations, processing, system development and risk

management services to ICC. Cross-margining of hedged positions exists with OCC.

inter-market spread
The sale of a given delivery month of a futures contract on one exchange and the simultaneous purchase of the same delivery month and a related futures contract on another exchange. *See* **TED spread, BED spread, crack spread.**

International Commodities Clearing House (ICCH)
Organization owned by the major UK banks that, through its London Clearing House division, clears both futures and options contracts for the London exchanges.

International Monetary Fund (IMF)
An organization of 126 countries created to (a) a promote international cooperation; (b) facilitate expansion and balanced growth of international trade; (c) promote exchange stability; (d) avoid competitive exchange depreciation; (e) assist in the establishment of a multi-national system of payments and elimination of foreign exchange restrictions; and (f) provide members with resources to correct short-term imbalance of payments. Created at Bretton Woods, New Hampshire, US, in July 1944.

International Petroleum Exchange (IPE)
The London oil exchange that trades a variety of cash or physical delivery futures and options contracts on crude and refined oil.

International Securities Market Association (ISMA)
The body that governs cross-border trading in securities, including eurobonds. A Designated Investment Exchange under the UK Financial Services Act. Formerly the AIBD.

inter-office or 'pre-market' trading (LME)
Dealings done outside ring sessions which must then be entered into the matching system for registration with the clearing house.

interval
The standard differential or interval between the exercise or strike prices of traded options contracts.

in-the-money option
An option having intrinsic value. A call option is in-the-money if its strike price is below the current price of the underlying contract. A put option is

in-the-money if its strike price is above the current price of the underlying contract. *See* **intrinsic value**.

intra-day margin call
A call made by the exchange or clearing house to clearing members and agents for additional initial margin to be made. This would reflect rapidly changing prices of greater magnitude than normal, and might occur in *fast markets*.

intra-market spread
A futures position where a near month contract is bought and a far month contract sold (or vice-versa) in the same underlying asset. The trade is one that looks for a profit in the changing relationship between the two contract prices and not a general rise or fall in the market. Because one position partly offsets the other then intra-market spread margins are lower than for each contract separately. *See also* **inter-delivery spread**.

intrinsic value
The amount by which an option is in-the-money or which would be realized if the option was immediately exercised, excluding premium cost. There are no negative figures for intrinsic value, it can only be as low as zero. If the holder has a call option exercisable at 100, and the market price is 110, a profit of 10 is realized upon exercise and intrinsic value is 10. If the market price is 90, the option is not exercised and it has zero intrinsic value. An option premium is comprised of intrinsic value and time value. *See* **in-the-money option**.

introducing broker (IB)
A person or organization that solicits, or accepts, orders to buy or sell futures contracts or commodity options but does not accept money or other assets from customers to support such orders. Any orders so obtained are passed to exchange members for execution.

inverted market
A futures market in which the relationship between two delivery months of the same commodity is abnormal with distant months cheaper than nearer months.

invisible supply
Uncounted stocks of a commodity in the hands of wholesalers, manufacturers, and producers that cannot be identified accurately; stocks outside commercial channels but theoretically available to the market.

invoice amount
The amount the clearing house invoices a buyer at delivery.

invoice amount (bond futures - LIFFE)
The principal invoice amount plus accrued interest. This is the full amount that the purchaser of a bond futures contract will be invoiced for upon delivery. It should not be confused with the principal invoice amount, which excludes accrued interest.

IOC
Immediate or cancel order.

IOM
The Index and Options Market of the CME. *See* Index and Option Market.

IPD
Investment Property Databank.

IPE
See **The International Petroleum Exchange of London.**

IR£
Textual abbreviation for Irish punt(s).

IRG
Interest rate guarantee.

Irish Futures and Options Exchange (IFOX)
Located in Dublin, it lists contracts on Irish gilts, three-month Dibor, and the ISEQ Index.

iron butterfly (options)
A straddle offset with a strangle.

ISDA
International Swap Dealers Association.

ISE
International Stock Exchange. The former name of the London Stock Exchange.

ISEQ
Irish Stock Exchange equity index.

island reversal
A technical analysis reversal pattern where the high or low is surrounded by gaps, usually exhaustion and breakaway gaps.

ISMA
International Securities Market Association.

ITL
Standard foreign exchange code for Italian lira (lire).

J

JEC
The Joint Exchanges Committee. A forum and lobbying body for the UK exchanges (LIFFE, LME, LCE, IPE and OML).

jelly rolls (options)
An arbitrage strategy comprised of a long synthetic asset position in one month and a short synthetic asset position in a different month, where both synthetic positions are done at the same exercise price. The value is the difference between the far and near synthetic markets. It is an arbitrage on the interest cost of carry and the difference in synthetic prices.

JGB
Japanese government bond. Most are of 10 year's maturity and pay coupons semi-annually.

job lot
Unit of trading smaller than the regular contract unit.

JPY
Standard foreign exchange code for Japanese yen.

K

Kansas City Board of Trade
A US exchange which lists Value Line equity stock index and wheat contracts.

kappa
See **vega**.

KCBT
See **Kansas City Board of Trade**.

kerb trading (LME)
Dealings in the ring or in the Room, and therefore done in the open market, between ring members, yet outside official or the afternoon 'unofficial', but still formalized market. Kerb dealings have significance in that they enable a ring member perhaps to complete business either interrupted by the bell in official trading, or which might have been too large in volume for a particular official market to have contained without an effect on prices. They are also a very large part of the essential flexibility of the LME, in that they provide the time, opportunity and market for the multiplicity of book-squaring transactions which ought to be done before a day's business is closed. The term 'kerb' dates from the time when dealers continued trading on the kerb outside the exchanges after they had closed.

key day reversal
A chart pattern that indicates a reversal of trend. It can only be identified after the reversal has occurred.

KLCE
See **Kuala Lumpur Commodity Exchange**.

knock-in option
See **barrier option**.

knock-out option
See **barrier option**.

Kobe Rubber Exchange
Located in Kobe, Japan, it lists a rubber futures contract.

KRE
See **Kobe Rubber Exchange**.

Kuala Lumpur Commodity Exchange
Located in Kuala Lumpur, Malaysia, it lists futures contracts on cocoa, palm oil, palm kernel oil, rubber and tin.

krugerrands
Gold coins issued largely for gold investment purposes by South Africa.

L

ladder (options)
A table top, i.e. buy a call, sell a higher strike call and sell an equally higher strike call, or sell a put, sell a higher strike put and buy an equally higher strike put.

lagging indicators
Market indicators showing the general direction of the economy and confirming, or denying the trend, implied by the leading indicators.

last notice day
The final day on which notices of intent to deliver on futures contracts may be issued.

last trading day
The final day under an exchange's rules during which trading may take place in a particular delivery futures month. Positions which have not been closed by the last trading day must be fulfilled by making or taking delivery of the physical commodity or financial instrument.

lates
Beyond the 15th of the month in respect of euronotes and CDs.

LAUTRO
Life Assurance and Unit Trust Regulatory Authority. (UK)

LCE
London Commodity Exchange.

LCH
London Clearing House.

leading indicators
Market indicators that signal the state of the economy for the coming months. Some of the leading indicators include average manufacturing work-week, lay-off rate of manufacturing workers, inflation-adjusted new orders for consumer goods and material, speed of delivery of new goods, rate of net business formation, contracts for plant and equipment, change in

inventories on hand, change in crude material prices, prices of stocks, change in total liquid assets, change in money supply.

LEAPS
Long-Term Equity AnticiPation securities. These are long-dated options listed on CBOE, PHLX amongst others.

leg
One side of a spread position.

lender option
A floor on a single period FRA.

lending
Sale of a nearby delivery date coupled with the simultaneous purchase of a more distant date (LME term).

LEPOs
Low exercise price options that trade on SOFFEX.

letter of renunciation
A form attached to an allotment letter that allots a rights issue to existing shareholders in the UK. Should shareholders wish to sell their rights other persons they will complete this letter.

leverage
The ability to control large monetary amounts of a financial instrument or commodity with a comparatively small amount of capital. *See also* **gearing**.

Libid
The London interbank bid or deposit rate, or the rate at which banks will bid for funds (deposits). *See also* **Libor**.

Libor
The London interbank offered rate, or the rate at which banks will offer funds. Rates exist for overnight, 1-month, 3-month, 6-month etc. out to 5 years, and for euro-currency deposits. Libid-Libor is the bid-offer spread. It is widely used as a reference rate for payments on floating-rate instruments.

licensed warehouse
A warehouse approved by an exchange from which a commodity may be delivered on a futures contract.

life of contract
Period between the beginning of trading in a particular futures contract and the expiration of trading. In some cases, this phrase denotes the period already passed in which trading has already occurred. For example, "the life of contract high is $2.50"

lifetime
The period during which the option can be exercised.

LIFFE
See **London International Financial Futures & Options Exchange**.

lifting a leg
Closing-out one half of a spread position. The trader is now uncovered to the extent of the remaining (open) commitment.

light oil
Density indicates the volume of higher value end-products that crude oil will yield from refining. Since the valuable products are low density, light crudes generally command higher prices than heavy crudes.

Limean
The average of Libid and Libor.

limit
See **limit order**.

limit (up or down)
The maximum price advance or decline from the previous day's settlement price permitted in one trading session.

limit move
A price that has advanced or declined the permissible limit during one trading session, as fixed by the rules of a contract market. More common in the US than the UK.

limit option
Also *trigger option*. *See* **barrier option**.

limit order
An order (also known as a *resting order*) given to a broker by a customer which has restrictions upon its execution. The customer specifies a stated price to buy at or below, or to sell at or above. If the order cannot be filled

in total the balance is normally kept for later execution and the order can only be executed if the market reaches or betters that price.

limit price
Largest permitted price fluctuation in a futures contract during a trading session, as fixed by the contract market's rules. Also known as *maximum price fluctuation*.

limits
See **position limit, price limit, variable limit**.

line chart
A chart of a single price for each trading period, usually the close price.

linkage
The ability to buy (sell) contracts on one exchange (such as the Chicago Mercantile Exchange) and later sell (buy) them on another exchange such as the Singapore International Financial Futures Exchange), i.e., mutual offset.

liquid
A characteristic of a security or commodity market with enough units outstanding to allow large transactions without a substantial change in price. Institutional investors are inclined to seek out liquid investments so that their trading activity will not influence the market price.

liquid market
A market condition where many participants are buying and selling substantial amounts without adversely moving the market in any significant way. An active market where selling and buying can be accomplished with minimal price concessions. This allows ease of trading.

liquidation
Any transaction that offsets or closes out a long or short position. *See* **buy in, closing**.

Liquidity Data Bank (LDB)
A computerized profile of CBOT market activity, used by technical traders to analyse price trends and develop trading strategies. There is a specialized display of daily volume data and time distribution of prices for every commodity traded on the Chicago Board of Trade.

Lit
Textual abbreviation for Italian lira (lire).

LME
See **London Metal Exchange**.

loan price
The price at which growers may obtain loans under government price support programmes. (US)

Loan Program
A US federal programme in which the government lends money at pre-announced rates to farmers and allows them to use the crops they plant for the upcoming crop year as collateral. Default on these loans is the primary method by which the government acquires stocks of agricultural commodities. (US)

loan rate
The amount lent per unit of a commodity to farmers. (US). See **Loan Program**.

local or local member
An individual floor trader who is also an exchange member. Further details will differ according to the exchange regulations and definitions including whether they may execute orders for other persons. They are often small, private, individual traders whose trading activities help provide liquidity in the market.

LOCH
London Options Clearing House. The former clearing house for LTOM. It was a wholly-owned subsidiary of the London Stock Exchange responsible for registering and settling all Stock Exchange traded options transactions.

locked
Either-way (same) prices (or yields) from brokers or dealers at which they will buy or sell a security.

locked-in profits/losses
Profits/losses in the future known with certainty now. Probably a result of a fully-covered hedged, spread or arbitrage position.

locked market
A market where trading has halted because prices have reached their daily limit move. Trading can resume the same day if prices come off their limit.

loco-London
Gold located in London vaults.

London Clearing House (LCH)
The clearing house for LIFFE, the London Commodity Exchange, IPE and the LME. It is owned by the major UK banks as a division of the ICCH. It provides a comprehensive service to members including registration, clearing, settlement, central banking and treasury, the administration of physical delivery and risk management.

London Code of Conduct
The Bank of England's rules that provide the principles and standards for the wholesale markets in sterling, foreign exchange and bullion. They are a statement of guidelines and best practice.

London Commodity Exchange (LCE)
Previously called London Fox, it lists agricultural and soft commodity contracts, including coffee, sugar, cocoa, potatoes, grains, etc.

London fixings
The gold fixing which provides customers with a single quoted price is undertaken at 10.30 and 15.00 hours.

London Fox
The London Futures and Options Exchange, being the former name of the London Commodity Exchange.

London good delivery
Physical delivery is made in bars conforming to specifications laid down by The London Bullion Market Association. London bars must be produced by an acceptable smelter and assayer. Sellers have no obligation to deliver bars of any particular brand; a purchaser has to accept good delivery bars.

London International Financial Futures & Options Exchange (LIFFE)
A UK exchange which lists futures on long-term interest rates (bonds), short term interest rates, and FTSE 100 Index. It lists options on its futures, on the FTSE 100 Index and on individual UK equities.

London Metal Exchange (LME)
A UK exchange which lists futures and options contracts on aluminium, recycled aluminium, copper, lead, tin, zinc and nickel in a unique system, each metal having set official trading times during the day.

London Span
The system used for assessing margin levels on UK futures and options exchanges. *See* **Span**.

London Stock Exchange
The UK Stock Exchange, listing UK gilts and fixed interest, domestic equities, international equities and traditional options. Trading via SEAQ and TOPIC price display systems, it has the status of a Recognized Investment Exchange.

long¹
One who has bought futures or options contracts or owns a financial instrument or cash commodity. An open purchased cash position or contract. Buying forward on the market. Holding more contracts to buy than to sell; to go long' means to increase purchases of contracts to buy.

long²
In terms of maturity a long maturity instrument or contract, i.e. long gilts with fifteen or more years to maturity.

long basis
See **long the basis**.

long bear spread
See **bear spread**.

long butterfly (options)
This is a strategy composed of a large number of options positions and hence there is a danger that commission costs can negate profits. It is also confusingly named, because comparing the profit to that of a long straddle or strangle, it would appear to better named as a short position. It is referred to as a long position because the maximum loss is limited. It is one of the few positions that may be entered into with advantage in the long-term option contracts. As a rule of thumb, it can be entered when the cost of the position is one-tenth or less of the difference between the lowest and intermediate exercise prices, and one twentieth if there exists an exercise price available between these two exercise prices. This is a rough guide and the price should be compared with theoretical values. Essentially, the position is a short straddle with the loss limited in both directions. It is composed of a long call at exercise price E_1, two short calls at E_2, and a long call at E_3, with $E_3 > E_2 > E_1$ and $E_3 - E_2 = E_2 - E_1$. Alternatively it may be constructed from a long put at E_1, two short puts at E_2, and a long put at E_3. Synthetic versions include long call at E_1, short put at E_2, short call at E_2, and long

call at E_3, or, long call at E_1, short call at E_2, short put at E_2 and long put at E_3. The profile is a flat loss to E_1, rising to E_2, falling to E_3, and then a flat loss above that. The maximum profit is thus at E_2, and maximum loss when the underlying is below E_1 or above E_3. Time decay works in favour of the position but is negligible until the final month. It is a trade based on the precision of market pricing.

long bull spread
See **bull spread**.

long call option
Used to support a very bullish view of the market, profits increase as the market rises, while downside risk is limited to the cost of the premium. If the market rises one can purchase the underlying asset at the exercise price and sell it at the higher market price. If the market falls a loss of the premium cost is incurred. The position will increase in value as volatility rises but is exposed to time value decay. It may be created synthetically from a long underlying instrument and a long put. The expiry profile is a flat line at premium cost below breakeven up to the exercise price, then an ascending line at 45°.

long condor (options)
A strategy comparable to a long butterfly, from which it differs in having four different exercise prices instead of three. The centre section is thus flat instead of an upward point. Its expiry profile is thus flat, ascending, flat, descending, flat.

long-dated forward
A forward foreign exchange contract with a maturity greater than one year. Some contracts may be as far out as 10 years.

long (going long)
Buying forward on the market, and thus being 'long' for a given date. May be a speculative position in anticipation of rising prices when the bought position may be closed-out by selling advantageously, or may be a market position taken against a contrary physical commitment.

long futures position
A bought future, based on an expectation of a rising market. Profit increases if the market rises, but losses mount if the futures market falls. Profits and losses are based on the difference between the entry price and exit price. The position is unaffected by volatility and has no decay characteristics. It

may be synthetically produced from a long call and short put with the same exercise price. The profile is a 45° upward sloping line.

long hedge
The purchase of a futures contract in anticipation of actual purchases in the cash market. *See also* **purchasing hedge**.

long-instrument conversion
See **option conversion**.

long option box
See **option box**.

long (over-bought)
Excess of purchases over sales.

long premium
A position where the holder has paid out more premium than received. A large price move in either direction will theoretically increase its value (subject to time value decay). It is long on volatility.

long put option
A bought put option. Used to support a very bearish view of the market. Profits increase as the market falls, while downside risk if the the market rises is limited to the cost of the premium. If the market falls a holder can sell the underlying asset at the exercise price, having held it or purchased it at a lower market price. If the market rises the premium cost is lost. The position will increase in value as volatility rises but is exposed to time value decay. It may be created synthetically from a short underlying instrument and a long call. The expiry profile is a falling 45° line to the exercise price and a flat line at premium cost below breakeven.

long rotated cylinder (options)
See **bear rotated cylinder**.

long straddle (options)
A strategy that may be employed when the underlying asset is priced near the common exercise price of the component options. Movement or increased volatility is expected, but the direction of movement is not known. This would be reflected in a quiet market that then starts to zigzag rapidly, suggesting a sharp movement. If the underlying moves such that the profit boundaries are breached clearly profits may be taken, but an increase in volatility alone will add value so that the position can be traded out at a

profit. Profits are open-ended for a large move, up or down. The position is constructed from a long call and a long put with a common exercise price. It may also be produced from two long puts and the long underlying asset, or two long calls and a short underlying asset. The expiry profile is open-ended profits in either direction, lines meeting at the maximum loss of the combined premium cost below breakdown at the common exercise price. The position is the classic volatility trade, but suffers from time decay. The position is usually done to initial delta neutrality and will thus only have equal numbers of calls and puts when the underlying is trading at the exercise price. As time decay accelerates, the position is adjusted to neutrality by profit taking. It is normally taken off well before expiry.

long strangle (options)
This strategy is one based on precision of option pricing. It is a volatility trade. Essentially it is a straddle with two exercise prices. It would be used when the underlying asset lay in the range of the two exercise prices and has been showing low volatility. If the asset moves significantly or becomes more volatile then profits are obtained, but if it remains stagnant less money is lost than with a straddle. It is formed from a long call and a long put, at exercise prices E_1 and E_2. The put or call options may be assigned to either exercise price where $E_2 > E_1$. (Where both options are out of the money the position is called a combination, and if in the money a guts. There is thus conflict here over which definition is a pure strangle). The expiry profile is a line falling downwards to the lower exercise price, flat between the two exercise prices at a loss of the combined premium cost, then an ascending line. Alternatively, it may be constructed by synthetically reproducing one of the options positions. It is all done to initial delta neutrality. Expiry profits are open ended for movements in both directions, but the spread is not usually held to expiry. Volatility is positive for the position. Time decay accelerates as options approach expiry, but not as rapidly as with a long straddle. However, to avoid the largest part of decay, the position is normally taken off before expiry.

long synthetic asset (options)
A long cash position created synthetically with a short put option and a long call option at the same exercise price.

long synthetic futures (split strike)
Can also be a zero-cost option. The strategy offers a bullish approach, as with a future, but is constructed with options and has a central area of limited gain or loss. It is constructed from a short put at one exercise price and a long call at a higher exercise price, the short premium income and long premium cost virtually offsetting each other. Profit increases as the

underlying rises above the long call exercise and losses are incurred if the underlying drops below the short put exercise price. Time decay works in the holder's favour if futures are lower, or against the holder if futures are higher. The profile is an upward sloping line, then flat between the two exercise prices, then rising again. *See also* **rotated cylinder**.

long-term interest rate contracts
Futures and options contracts on long-term interest rates are contracts on long maturity bonds. The futures contracts are for notional bonds of a stated coupon and maturity range, such as LIFFE's long gilt future, which is based on a 9% notional gilt of 10-15 years' maturity. In this way, a range of bonds that satisfy exchange criteria in terms of maturity, liquidity, etc., are deliverable. The delivery price is established from the futures closing price as adjusted by a price factor unique to each actual bond, and for each future delivery month, reflecting the fact that bonds with higher coupons than the notional bond will be worth relatively more and bonds with lower coupons worth less. There will always be one bond that will be the cheapest to deliver when comparing the delivery receipts with the cash market price. Compared with all other deliverable bonds, it will provide the greatest profit or least loss at delivery. It should be noted that this futures contract usually provides the seller with a choice of delivery day within the delivery month. With a positive yield curve, delivery will usually be effected late in the month, and with an inverted curve it will be effected early. If the curve is likely to change shape there is thus an implicit option in the futures price. Long-term interest-rate options are options on the futures contract. The tick size may sometimes be smaller than for the future.

long-term interest rate futures
These are bond futures on instruments such as long gilts, Treasury bonds, Bunds, BTPs, JGBs etc. The contracts are on notional instruments, but delivery is effected with actual bonds that meet eligibility requirements as set by the exchange in terms of maturity, liquidity, coupon etc. Because the actual bonds will differ in value from the notional instruments the delivery is invoiced at the exchange settlement price multiplied by a price factor that is unique to the bond delivered. *See also* **price factor, invoice amount** and **principal invoice amount**.

long Texas 'hedge' (options)
A long underlying position geared up with the addition of a long call. This is a speculative position and shows very geared profits if the underlying rises. It is not a hedged position.

long the basis
Long the asset underlying the futures contract and short the future. If basis decreases the position may make money, if it increases the position loses money. *See also* **short the basis**.

lookback option
An option that gives the holder the right to buy (call) at the lowest price or sell (put) at the highest price the underlying has traded during the option life. Lookback options offer the opportunity to deal at the most favourable price, buying in at the lowest level or selling out at the top. An ordinary option has to be exercised at a point in time and a potential later profit may be foregone. Consequently, lookback options can be up to 100% more expensive than standard options (naturally depending on volatility and maturity of the option), so purchasers need to be sure that volatility or movement will justify the cost. They are actually two options working against each other, an option on the exercise price and an option on the underlying. Option pricing theory only allows the pricing of each separately, so although they offset each other it is not known how to price this cheaper and hence they are charged as two option premiums.

lookback strike options
These set the strike rate for calls as the lowest, or for puts as the highest, level of the underlying asset over a period of time less than the final option maturity.

lot
The minimum value of the underlying that may be transacted in a contract, i.e. 5 tonnes of coffee, £50,000 nominal of gilts etc. In essence, the futures contract.

lotting factor
The ratio of contract volume traded per executed transaction, in any given contract.

low
The lowest price of the day for a particular contract. *See also* **high** for further detail.

LPG
Liquid petroleum gas.

LSE
London Stock Exchange.

LTOM
The London Stock Exchange's London Traded Options Market that listed equity and index options. This merged into the new London International Financial Futures and Options Exchange in early 1992. Confusingly, the logo of the new exchange LIFFOE incorporates the LIFFE letters with LTOM given less prominence and the exchange is still referred to as LIFFE.

M

'Mae West' (options)
An obscure strategy that produces an inverted 'W' profile.

maintenance margin
A sum, usually smaller than, but part of, the original margin, which must be maintained on deposit at all times. If a customer's equity in any futures position drops to, or under, the maintenance margin level, the broker must issue a margin call for the amount of money required to restore the customer's equity in the account to the original margin level.

managed account
See **discretionary account**.

Manila International Futures Exchange (MIFE)
Located in Manila, Philippines, it lists futures on coffee, copra, dry cocoons, soybeans, sugar and currencies.

Marché à Terme International de France S.A. (MATIF)
Located in Paris, the exchange lists contracts on long- and short-term interest rates and stock indices. The commodities division lists coffee, sugar, cocoa and potato contracts.

Marché des Options Négociables des Paris (MONEP)
The Paris options exchange listing contracts on individual equities and the CAC-40 stock index.

margin
A cash amount of funds that must be deposited with the broker (and/or clearing house) for each futures or options contract as a guarantee of fulfilment of the contract. Also called a *security deposit*. It is subject to be increased or decreased as the market changes. A margin deposit is effectively a performance bond to make sure that the holder of a losing contract meets their bargain.

margin (currency asset markets)
The stated margin (or spread) is expressed as a percentage, added to or subtracted from a reference interest rate (e.g. six-month Libor) to establish the coupon of a floating-rate instrument.

margin call
A call from a clearing house to a clearing member, or from a brokerage firm to a customer, to bring margin deposits up to a required minimum level.

market difference (LME)
The margin on prompt date calculated from the difference between the contract price and the official settlement price.

market going better (or up)
Terminology used in bond markets when prices are rising and interest rates are falling.

market going worse (or down)
Terminology used in bond markets when prices are falling and interest rates are rising.

market-if-touched (MIT)
Also called a *board order*. This order becomes a market order if the contract month trades, or is offered at or below the limit price in the case of a buy order, or if the contract trades at or is bid at or above the limit price in the case of a sell order. A buy MIT order and a buy limit order are both placed below the market, whilst a sell MIT order and a sell limit are both placed above the market. This differs from a stop order in that a buy stop is placed above the market and a sell stop is placed below the market. The actual difference between a limit order and a MIT order is that a limit order must be filled at the limit price or better, whereas an MIT order may be filled at any price once the trigger price is hit.

Market Information Data Inquiry System (MIDIS-Touch)
Daily Chicago Board of Trade price, volume, and open interest data accessible by telephone.

market-maker
A individual or organization which, in exchange for reduced dealing fees and other concessions, commits in certain securities, contracts or markets to continuously make two-way prices (i.e. bids and offers) at an agreed minimum spread differential and for an agreed minimum volume, during market hours.

market-maker fee
The reduced exchange fee levied on market-makers in return for the service that they provide to the market.

market-maker spread
The minimum price range between bid and offer to which a market-maker is committed.

market on close (MOC)
This type of order is placed during the trading session to be executed as a limit order. However, if the limit is not reached during the session, the order becomes a market order on the close.

market order
An order to buy or sell a futures contract at whatever price is obtainable at the time it is received in the ring or pit.

market risk
The exposure that a trader has between the perceived execution of a trade and the actual matching and registration of a trade.

market price
See **clean price**.

Market Price Reporting and Information System (MPRIS)
The Chicago Board of Trade's computerized price-reporting system.

market reporter
A person employed by the exchange, and located in or near the trading pit who records prices as they occur during trading.

mark-to-market
Process of revaluing futures and options positions daily using settlement prices to obtain profit or loss and hence variation margin.

matched trade
A transaction with all details as to contract type, delivery month, price, volume, obligation and counterparty, properly identified and passed to the clearing house for registration.

matching system
The system operated by or on behalf of an exchange for the matching and confirmation of contracts. Contracts are paired sellers to buyers in order to be confirmed by each before registration with the clearing house. They are then separated into contracts between each party with the clearing house alone.

MATIF
See **Marché à Terme International de France.**

maturity[1]
Period within which a futures contract can be settled by delivery of the actual commodity.

maturity[2]
The period between the first notice day and the last trading day of a commodity futures contract.

maturity[3]
The due date of a loan, note, bond, or, in the USA a mortgage-backed security.

MBS
Mortgage-backed security.

ME
See **Montreal Exchange.**

measuring gap
A gap in the price pattern that occurs when a trend is under way. It signals a continuation of the trend and is usually not filled, although it may be partially filled.

MEFF Renta Fija
Located in Barcelona, Spain, it lists contracts on Spanish government bonds and notes and Mibor.

MEFF Renta Variable
Located in Madrid Spain, it lists Spanish stock options and contracts on the IBEX 35 stock index.

member's fee
See **exchange fee.**

Mercado de Futuros y Opciones S.A. (MERFOX)
Located in Buenos Aires, Argentina, it lists contracts on cattle.

Mercato Italiano Futures (MIF)
Located in Rome, Italy, it lists BTP futures.

MERFOX
See **Mercado de Futuros y Opciones**.

Mexican hat (options)
An obscure strategy that is a more geared up version of a butterfly.

MGE
See **Minneapolis Grain Exchange**.

MGMI
Metallgezellschaft Metals Index. A base metal index that has traded as a contract on London Fox.

Mibid
Madrid interbank bid rate.

Mibor
Madrid interbank offered rate.

MidAm
See **MidAmerica Commodity Exchange**.

MidAmerica Commodity Exchange
Located in Chicago, USA, it lists contracts on currencies, precious metals, live cattle, live hogs, soybeans, grains, T-bills, T-notes and T-bonds.

MIF
See **Mercato Italiano Futures**.

MIFE
See **Manila International Futures Exchange**.

mine (foreign exchange and currency deposit markets)
The dealer takes the 'spot' or 'forward', whichever has been quoted by the counterparty. NB, This is a very dangerous term and must be qualified by the amount involved.

minimax
A collar with a tight range, or, in foreign exchange markets a strategy for reducing cost by foregoing some gain. An option buyer also sells an option at a different strike price.

minimum price fluctuation or movement
Set by the rules of the exchange, this is the minimum unit by which the price of a future or option can fluctuate per trade. *See* **tick**.

minimum rate
In the context of floating-rate paper, that interest rate below which the coupon may not be fixed.

minimum size
The minimum contract volume to which a market-maker commits.

minimum spread
See **market-maker spread**.

Minneapolis Grain Exchange
A US exchange which lists contracts on wheat, oats and frozen shrimps.

mismatch trade
A transaction wherein both parties agree to the principle that a trade took place, but that one or more of the details of the transaction are in dispute.

MIT
Market-if-touched order. Also called a *board order*.

MKT
Market order.

MLC
Meat and Livestock Commission. (UK)

MMI
Major Market Index. A US stock index traded on CBOT, Amex and EOE.

mnemonic
The abbreviation of a members company used on a trading badge.

MOC
Market on close order.

Mofex
Mercado de Opciones. Now closed, it listed options on Spanish government bonds, Mibor-90 and FIEX 35.

MONEP
See **Marché des Opciones Négociables des Paris**.

money-back option
An option guaranteed to repay at least the original option premium at expiry. This results in the gearing being greatly reduced compared with a standard option.

money supply
The amount of money in the economy, consisting primarily of currency in circulation plus deposits in banks. It is variously measured as M1, M2, M3, M4, M5, etc.

Montreal Exchange (ME)
Located in Montreal, Canada, it lists contracts on bankers' acceptances, bonds and equities.

mortgage-backed security
A bond backed by a pool of mortgages. First traded in America such securities now exist in Denmark, UK and Japan.

moving average charts
A statistical price analysis method of recognizing different price trends. A moving average is calculated by adding the prices for a predetermined number of days and then dividing by the number of days. Cross-overs of the average and the price, or a short and long moving average indicate buy and sell signals.

moving average cross-over
A chart signal. When the price plot of the shorter moving average rises above a longer moving average, a buy signal is generated. The reverse situation indicates a sell signal.

MQP
Mandatory quote period.

MSCI
Morgan Stanley Capital Index (Europe).

municipal bonds
Debt securities issued by state and local governments, and special districts and counties.

multi-currency
An expression to denote that a facility can be drawn in different currencies.

multi-index option
An option that gives the holder the right to buy the asset that performs best out of a number of assets, i.e. a call on the best performing index. The indices would all be rebased for comparison and the currency may or may not have a fixed exchange rate. This product was introduced by Mitsubishi Finance.

mutual offset
The ability to open a contract on one exchange and close it on another, for example, Treasury bond futures on CME and SIMEX.

MYR
Standard foreign exchange code for Malaysian ringgit(s).

N

Nagoya Stock Exchange
Located in Nagoya, Japan, it lists a 25-Stock Index option.

naked writer
A person who writes a short option position and is not covered by possession of or need for the underlying asset, i.e., a short call option position where the underlying asset is not held or a short put option position where the underlying asset is not intended to be purchased in the future.

narrow tape
The tape band used to carry an exchange's own price feed as opposed to a commercial quote vendor's broad band tape.

NASD
National Association of Securities Dealers, in the US.

NASDAQ
National Association of Securities Dealers Automated Quotations System.

National Futures Association (NFA)
An industry-wide, industry-supported, self-regulatory organization for futures and options markets. The primary responsibilities of the NFA are to enforce ethical standards and customer protection rules, screen futures professionals for membership, audit and monitor professionals for financial and general compliance rules, and provide for arbitration of futures-related disputes. (US)

nearby delivery
The nearest active month of delivery on a futures market.

nearby (delivery) month
The futures contract month closest to expiration. Also referred to as *spot month*.

negative yield curve
See **yield curve**.

negotiable warehouse receipt
A legal document issued by a warehouse describing and guaranteeing the existence of a specific quantity (and sometimes a specific grade) of a commodity stored in the warehouse.

negotiated options
Options on gilt-edged stock intended for the professional markets. They have a minimum value of £100,000 nominal of gilts into which they may be exercised and a maximum life of 2 years. The exercise price, premium, size, maturity are all negotiated and no margin is required. They may only be closed out with the original counterparty and there is no secondary market. The structure is governed by the rules of the London Stock Exchange.

net position
The difference between the open long contracts and the open short contracts held by a person or institution in any one financial instrument or commodity.

neutral spread
A delta neutral spread but may also mean the number of long contracts equals the number of short contracts.

New Time
UK Stock Exchange 'New Time' dealings may be undertaken only by agreement between both parties, in the last two days of the account, and are then settled as if done during the following account.

New York Cotton Exchange (NYCE)
A US exchange which lists futures and options on cotton and frozen concentrated orange juice. Its financial division FINEX lists contracts on currencies and Treasury notes.

New York Futures Exchange (NYFE)
A US exchange which lists NYSE Index, CRB Index and US Treasury bond contracts.

New York Mercantile Exchange (NYMEX)
A US exchange which lists oil, gas and precious metal contracts.

New York Stock Exchange (NYSE)
Located on Wall Street, it lists equity and NYSE Index contracts.

New Zealand Futures and Options Exchange Ltd. (NZFOE)
Located in Auckland, New Zealand, it lists contracts on currencies, equities, government bonds, 90-day accepted bills and the Forty Index of shares.

NFA
National Futures Association. (US)

Nikkei- 225
The Nikkei Stock Average on 225 Japanese equities traded on the Tokyo Stock Exchange. Derivatives contracts are available on Osaka, CME and Singapore.

nil paid
A new issue of shares, usually made as a result of a rights issue, on which no payment has yet been made.

NKr
Textual abbreviation for Norwegian krone(r).

NLG
Standard foreign exchange code for Netherlands guilder(s).

NOK
Standard foreign exchange code for Norwegian krone(r).

No 2 fuel oil
A distillate fuel oil for domestic heating.

NOB
Notes over bonds. US Treasury notes and Treasury bond futures spread, tradeable on CBOT.

nominal price
Price quotations for a futures period in which no actual trading took place, usually an average of bid and asked prices.

nominal value
The face value of a financial instrument. In the case of bonds this is usually 100 and all price quotes are expressed against this, i.e., 96 meaning 96% of the nominal value. Also known as *par value* or *redemption value*.

non-clearing member
A member of an exchange that is not a clearing member of the exchange's

clearing house. All non-clearing member trades must clear through a clearing agent that is a clearing member of the clearing house.

non-member traders
Speculators and hedgers who trade on the exchange through a member but do not hold exchange memberships.

note futures
Futures on US Treasury notes. They operate the same way as long-term interest rate or bond futures.

not held order
If a broker fails to execute an order at a price in accordance with a client's instructions because of market movements he or she is not held to fulfilling that order. In London many brokers operate on a held order basis and would see themselves obligated to fill it (thus taking any loss themselves).

notional contract
A contract based on a basket of standardized maturity instruments but with certain variable factors which determine the contract to be an index rather than instrument specific.

notice day[1]
A day on which notices of intent to deliver pertaining to a specified delivery month may be issued. *See* **delivery notice**.

notice day[2]
According to Chicago Board of Trade rules, the second day of the three-day delivery process when the clearing corporation matches the buyer with the oldest reported long position to the delivery seller and notifies both parties. *See* **first notice day**.

novation
The principal of operation of a clearing house whereby it becomes the counterparty to each trade.

NSE
See **Nagoya Stock Exchange**.

NYBID
New York interbank bid rate.

NYBOR
New York interbank offered rate.

NYCE
See **New York Cotton Exchange**.

NYFE
See **New York Futures Exchange**.

NYMEX
See **New York Mercantile Exchange**.

NYSE
See **New York Stock Exchange**.

NZ$
Textual abbreviation for New Zealand dollar(s).

NZD
Standard foreign exchange code for New Zealand dollar(s).

NZFOE
See **New Zealand Futures and Options Exchange Ltd**.

O

OAT
Obligations Assumilables de Trésor or fungible French government bonds. They are available at fixed-rate for maturities of 7, 10, 15 and 25 years, and variable-rate at 12 years. Coupons are payable annually.

OBO
Order book official (US).

OBX
Oslo Stock Exchange index of 25 Norwegian equities.

OCC
Options Clearing Corporation. A Clearing body for exchange options in the US and a registered clearing agency and self-regulatory organization under the jurisdiction of the SEC. It is owned equally by AMEX, CBOE, NASD, NYSE, PSE and PHLX.

OCO
One cancels another order.

offer
Indicates a willingness to sell a futures or options contract, or other asset, at a given price.

offer into bids
The reverse situation to bid into offers.

offer price
The price or yield of a security at which a vendor is willing to sell. Also called *ask price*. Marked on some exchange price displays with an (A).

offset[1]
Liquidation of a long or short position by the opposite transaction. The sale offsets a long position; the purchase offsets a short position.

offset[2]
Matching total long with total short contracts for the purpose of determining a net long or net short position.

offset[3]
Non-competitively matching one customer's sell order, a practice that is permissible only when executed under governing regulations.

'off the run'
An old issue in which the market shows less interest. See **'on the run'**.

OFT
The Office of Fair Trading. (UK)

OGE
See **Osaka Grain Exchange**.

OIE
Overseas Investment Exchange. (UK)

OIP
Official index period.

OML
Former name of OMLX.

OMLX
See **OMLX, The London Securities and Derivatives Exchange**.

OMLX, The London Securities and Derivatives Exchange (OMLX)
The Swedish option market operating in London as a Recognized Investment Exchange. It lists contracts on Swedish equities, the OMX Index, T-bills, government bonds and mortgage bonds. See also **OM Stockholm Fondkommission AB**.

OM Stockholm Fondkommission AB (OM)
Swedish option market listing equity, equity index, and interest rate futures and options. It is linked in to OMLX to form a large single market. It has links with some of EOE's contracts.

omega[1]
The currency risk resulting when an option contract transaction has to be accounted for in a different currency.

omega[2]
Same as **vega**.

omnibus account
An account which can accommodate by deed of authorized discretion a number of trading accounts on a pooled basis.

OMS
OMLX's margin system.

OMX
Option Market Index, the Swedish equity index. It is based on the 30 most heavily-traded stocks on the Stockholm Stock Exchange.

one cancels the other (OCO) order
An order which gives the broker an instruction to fill one of two alternative orders. As soon as one is executed the other is cancelled. It may be used to sell out a position at a stated profit or at a limited loss.

one touch (all-or-nothing) options
Digital options that pay out a fixed amount ('all') if, at any time during the life of the option the underlying asset reaches a defined level. These offer a lower outlay to the buyer than a conventional option. *See also* **digital options, barrier options.**

on the run[1]
With respect to Treasury bills, the most recently issued 3-, 6- or 12-month bills. Also refers to top banks' issues of CDs.

on the run[2]
A recent issue, usually bonds, in which there is still interest because it is new. *See* **'off the run'**.

OPEC
Organization of Petroleum Exporting Countries, emerged as the major petroleum pricing power in 1973, when the ownership of oil production in the Middle East transferred from the operating companies to the governments of the producing countries or to their national oil companies. Members are Algeria, Ecuador, Gabon, Indonesia, Iran, Iraq, Kuwait, Libya, Nigeria, Qatar, Saudi Arabia, the United Arab Emirates and Venezuela.

on track
In the USA, a type of deferred delivery in which the price is set f.o.b seller's location and the buyer agrees to pay freight costs to the seller's nominated destination.

open contracts
Contracts which have been bought or sold without the transaction being closed or completed by subsequent sale or purchase, or by making or taking actual delivery of the commodity, or exercising the option.

opening order
An order that has to be executed within the opening range but not necessarily at the opening price. If the broker cannot achieve this it is cancelled. The order will specify a price and the broker will attempt to get that price or better. *See also* **opening sale** and **opening purchase**.

opening range
A range of prices at which buy and sell transactions take place during the opening of the market.

opening, the
The period at the beginning of the trading session officially designated by the exchange during which all transactions are considered made 'at the opening.

open interest
The total number of futures or options contracts of a given underlying instrument that have not yet been offset and closed by an opposite futures or options transaction nor fulfilled by delivery of the cash or commodity or option exercise. Each open transaction has a buyer and a seller, but for calculation of open interest, only one side of the contract is counted.

opening procedure
The market procedure to establish the opening level of a particular contract.

opening purchase
An order that establishes a new long position.

opening sale
An order that establishes a new short position.

open order
An open order is an order that remains in force until the customer explicitly cancels the order or until the futures contract expires.

open position (foreign exchange and currency deposit markets)
Difference between total spot and forward purchases and sales in a currency on which an exchange risk is run.

open market operation
The buying and selling of government securities—Treasury bills, notes, and bonds—by the Bank of England (UK) or Federal Reserve (US) etc. to supplement its control of the market.

open outcry
Trading conducted by called out bids and offers across a trading floor. Bids and offers must be audible to all participants in the trading arena. Usually accompanied by hand signals.

option
A legally binding agreement that confers the right, but not the obligation, to the holder to buy (in the case of a call option) or sell (in the case of a put option) an underlying asset (which may be a financial instrument, commodity, or futures contract) at a price agreed now (the exercise or strike price) by a specified expiry date in the future (if it is an American-style option) or on a specified date in the future (if it is a European-style option). The writer or seller of the option has the obligation to fulfil the contract if the holder wishes to exercise the option (take up the rights). This option is obtained in exchange for payment of a premium. There are exchange traded options available as well as over-the-counter varieties.

option box
An option box is a locked-in trade or arbitrage trade. The value at expiry is entirely independent of the price of the underlying asset and the whole trade is undertaken in order to make an arbitrage profit out of market mispricing. Option boxes, conversions and reversals are more commonly undertaken to 'lock' all or part of a portfolio by buying or selling to create the missing 'legs' of the position and guarantee a price. As such, the expiry profile is flat at a locked price. They are alternatives to closing out positions at unfavourable prices. A *long* option box is a synthetic long asset at the low exercise price and a synthetic short asset at the higher exercise price. It is a long call and a short put at one exercise price and a short call and a long put at a higher exercise price. It is also equivalent to a bull put spread and a bear call spread. The position value is the difference in exercise prices. A *short* option box is a synthetic short asset at the lower exercise price and a synthetic long asset at the higher exercise price, that is, a long put and a short call at one exercise price, and a short put and long call at a higher exercise price. It is also equivalent to a bull call spread and a bear put spread. The position value is the low exercise price less the high exercise price.

option buyer
A purchaser of either a call or put option. Option buyers receive the right, but not the obligation, to assume an underlying cash or futures position. Also referred to as a *holder*.

option conversion
Refer to option box. A conversion is the same position as a long option box except that a long underlying asset is used in place of a synthetic version. It is a long put, short call and long underlying asset. The position value is zero, its 'price' is the asset price + put premium - exercise price - call premium. *See also* **option reversal**.

option-dated forward contract
A forward foreign exchange contract with an option to select the date of the exchange.

option forward
See **option-dated forward contract**.

option group
Options in the same three-month interval and with the same exercise price.

option holder
Someone who has bought an option.

option on a cap
See **caption**.

option on a floor
See **floortion**.

option on a future
An option, the exercise of which results in a futures position rather than a claim directly on an underlying security or asset. The exercise of a call results in a long futures position for the buyer (a short position for the seller, or writer). The exercise of a put results in a short futures position for the buyer (a long position for the writer).

option on Libor
A cap or floor referenced to Libor.

option on an option
See **compound option**.

option premium
The going (market) price for an option.

option reversal
Refer to option box. A reversal is the same position as a short option box except that a short underlying asset is used in place of a synthetic version. It is a short put, long call and short underlying asset. The position value is zero, its 'price' is the asset price + exercise price + call premium - put premium.

option spread
The simultaneous purchase and sale of one or more options contracts, futures, and/or cash positions.

option strategies
Options may be thought of as building blocks which, together with the underlying asset, may be used to build many different strategies designed to take advantage of a particular view, requirements, or hedge operation. These are listed here under the strategy name described as the bull or bear, or long or short version. *See* bull or bear, long or short, call, put, spread, straddle, strangle, butterfly, condor, ratio spread, ratio backspread, table top, synthetic future, cylinder, fence, rotated cylinder, combination, guts, box, conversion, reversal, Mexican hat, 'Mae West', 'Texas hedge', jelly roll. Such strategies are usually vertical spreads, but there are also time spreads and diagonal spreads.

option writer
Originator of an option; an exchange member who sells an option contract.

original margin
The margin needed to cover a specific new position.

orders
See under the specific order type.

order book official (US)
The exchange official responsible for executing limit orders in a trading post.

ordinary share
The most common form of shares or equity. The ordinary shareholders are the owners of a company. Holders receive dividends the amount of which will vary with the profitability of the company and the recommendations of

the directors. Shareholders will also be looking for a rise in the value of their shares as the company prospers. Shareholders are entitled to receive the Annual Report and to vote at shareholders' meetings. Many exchanges list option contracts on ordinary shares and a few list futures on individual shares.

origins
The national or regional source of production or growth of commodities.

Osaka 50
A Japanese equity index comprising 50 stocks.

Osaka Grain Exchange (OGE)
Located in Osaka, Japan, it lists futures on red beans and imported soybeans.

Osaka Securities Exchange (OSE)
Located in Osaka, Japan, it lists Nikkei 225 options and Osaka 50 futures.

Osaka Sugar Exchange
Located in Osaka, Japan, it lists raw sugar contracts.

OSE
See **Osaka Securities Exchange**.

Oslo Stock Exchange
A Norwegian exchange which lists contracts on bonds, equities and equity indices.

OTC
See **over-the-counter**.

ÖTOB Clearing Bank Aktiengesellschaft (ÖTOB)
Located in Vienna, Austria, this exchange lists contracts on equities, government bonds and the Austrian Traded Index (ATX) stock index.

OTT warrant
Over-the-top warrant.

out
The market term given to a pit trader indicating that an previously given order has been cancelled.

out of position
See **position**$^{2.}$

out-of-the-money
A situation where the market price of a futures contract is below the exercise price of a call, or above the exercise price of a put. The option has no intrinsic value.

outperformance option
See **rainbow option**.

outright or outright forward
A forward.

out trade
A trade made on an exchange that cannot be processed due to conflicting terms reported by the two parties to the trade.

over-and-out option
See **up and out option** under **barrier option**.

over-and-out warrant
See **over-the-top warrant**.

overbought
A technical opinion that the market price has risen too steeply and too fast in relation to underlying fundamental factors.

overbroked
A general term indicating that there is greater capacity in an exchange or market to execute business than there are customers for such services.

Overseas Investment Exchange
An exchange outside the UK that wishes to carry on a market in the UK may be recognized by the Treasury directly as having systems comparable to a UK RIE. NASDAQ and the Sydney Futures and Options Exchange are so recognized.

oversold
A technical opinion that the market price has declined too steeply and too fast in relation to underlying fundamental factors.

over-the-counter
The off-exchange markets between principals and with counterparties. The deals are tailor-made and not standardized.

over-the-top option
See up-and-out option under barrier option.

over-the-top warrant
A warrant with the same features as an up-and-out option. *See* under **barrier option**.

overwrite
Sale of calls against an existing long underlying position.

P

P & S (purchase and sale) statement
A statement sent by a commission house to customers when their futures, or options on futures, position has changed, showing the number of contracts bought or sold, the prices at which the contracts were bought or sold, the gross profit or loss, the commission charges, and the net profit or loss on the transactions. (US)

Pacific Stock Exchange (PSE)
Located in Los Angeles and San Francisco, it lists options on equities and the Wilshire Small Cap stock index.

paper[1]
Generic term referring to securities.

paper[2]
Client orders coming to the market.

paper market
A market in forwards, futures or options as distinct from the physical cash commodity market.

paper profit
The profit that would be realized if open contracts were liquidated.

par
100% of the nominal value of a debt security.

par (foreign exchange and currency deposit markets)
Price is the same on both sides of the swap.

parity[1]
A theoretically equal relationship between farm product prices, and all other prices. In US farm programme legislation, parity provides a yardstick to measure the purchasing power of farmers.

parity[2]
Another term for intrinsic value.

partial fill
An order that has only been executed in part.

participating cap
The simultaneous purchase of an out-of-the-money cap and sale of a lesser amount of in-the-money floors. Since the floors are worth more than the caps a zero-cost combination can be purchased. The whole position becomes profitable if rates fall. The gains are less than with a straightforward cap but no premium is expended.

participating forward[1]
Like a synthetic future but where the options sold finance the options purchased. Thus the call (put) options purchased must be out-of-the-money whilst those puts (calls) sold must be in-the-money, resulting in a low or zero cost position. So, if hedging against a falling price short the synthetic, sell in-the-money calls and buy more out-of-the-money puts. If the asset price rises only partial advantage can be taken, but cover is provided if it falls. This position overall approximates the long asset, plus a short asset, plus the extra puts, leaving it net the extra puts. It is like an asset, hedged with a forward, plus an option.

participating forward[2]
A second definition also known as a *profit-sharing forward*, which is an adaptation of the range forward in which only a floor is fixed. In place of a premium, the holder agrees to pass a percentage of any gain to the seller. This seller's participation rate varies in direct proportion to the level of the floor—a low participation rate gives a low floor, and vice versa. The buyer has the choice of participation rate and floor. Based on the choice made the seller then fixes the other variable.

participation rate
See **participating forward**[2].

participating option
An option where the buyer foregoes a certain percentage of potential profits in return for a reduced premium.

pass-through security
Securities whose interest and principal payments on mortgages are passed on to the certificate holder after dealer service fees are deducted.

path-dependent option
An option with a payout directly related to movements in the price of the

underlying asset during the life of the option, rather than the price at a point in time before expiry (American) or at expiry (European). As such the category includes average rate (Asian) options, Atlantic options, barrier options and lookback options.

Payment-in-Kind (PIK) Program
A US government programme in which farmers who comply with a voluntary acreage-control programme and set aside an additional percentage of acreage specified by the government receive certificates that can be redeemed for government-owned stocks of grain.

pay-up
The additional cash outlay incurred on the sale of one block of securities and purchase of another. *See* **take-out**.

PBOT
See **Philadelphia Board of Trade**.

peak
A high point in market price activity.

pennant
A chart continuation pattern that lasts one to three weeks.

percentage retracement
A reversal of a price move up or down. Certain percentages of retracement form key support or resistance levels, while extreme retracements may signal a 100% retracement will take place.

performance bond margin
The amount of money deposited by both a buyer and seller of a futures contract or an options seller (and perhaps buyer as well) to ensure performance of the terms of the contract. Margin is not a payment of equity or down payment on the commodity itself, but rather it is a security deposit. *See* **customer margin** and **clearing margin**.

perpetual bond
A bond with no pre-determined redemption date. Many have a date after which they may be redeemed by the issuer, such as UK government 2% Consols (1923 and after). Effectively, they have an open-ended issuers' call.

Philadelphia Board of Trade (PBOT)
A US exchange which lists currency futures.

Philadelphia Stock Exchange (PHLX)
A US exchange which lists options on a currencies, equities, and a number of stock indices.

PHLX
See **Philadelphia Stock Exchange**.

PHP
Standard foreign exchange code for Philippine peso(s).

physical delivery
Settlement of a contract by the delivery or receipt of a financial instrument or commodity.

pick-up
The gain in yield resulting from the sale of one block of securities and the purchase of another *See* **give-up**.

pin risk
The risk to a short option position writer that, at expiry, the price of the underlying will equal the exercise price. The writer will not then know whether or not the option will be exercised.

pip
1/100 of one percent of the nominal value of a security, e.g. $0.10 per $1000.

pit
Place where futures are traded by open outcry on the floor of an exchange.

pit broker
See **floor broker**.

pit card
The trading card used by traders to detail all elements of a trade whilst in the pit.

pitch
Conventionally an options trading area, analogous with a futures pit.

pitch official
A member of the exchange staff appointed to ensure orderly trading on the floor of an exchange.

pit observer
An exchange official responsible for updating price information, monitoring trading, and acting as arbitrator and regulator.

PL480
Public Law 480. In the 1950s, the US passed a series of trade and aid agreements with countries with inconvertible currencies (such as India). It said that US earnings (in rupees) would be held in that country and lent to it to enable it to purchase agricultural exports from the US. This has an impact on the soybean oil exports of the US to Pakistan for example.

PLO
Public limit order. A means of posting an order on LTOM.

PLOB
Public limit order board. The board for PLOs.

plus
(+) 1/64. Used in some bond markets such as US Treasury bonds. These are normally quoted in 1/32nds, i.e. 92-15 is a price of 92 and 15/32nds. A quote of 92-15+ would be 92 and 31/64ths.

PMB
Potato Marketing Board.

point[1]
Minimum price unit in which a commodity price is quoted, or minimum price movement of a future. *See* tick.

point[2]
One per cent of the nominal value of a security; i.e. one hundred basis points.

point-and-figure charts
Charts that show price changes of a minimum amount plotted independent of the time period involved. 'X's mark an upward move and 'O's a downward move.

point clerk
A floor clerk who signals or relays trading information from the edge of a futures pit to booth staff and phone brokers.

POM (public order member)
An exchange member authorized to transact business on behalf of clients, but not to clear such business.

pop-up option
See **up-and-in option** under **barrier option**.

pork bellies
One of the major cuts of the hog (pig) carcass that, when cured, becomes bacon.

position^1
A market commitment. A buyer of a futures or options contract is said to have a long position and, conversely, a seller of futures or options contract is said to have a short position. A position is having an exposure in the market by either buying or selling derivatives or the cash market asset or commodity.

position^2
'In position' refers to a commodity located where it can readily be moved to another point or delivered on a futures contract. Commodities not so situated are 'out of position'. Soya beans in Mississippi are out of position for delivery in Chicago, but in position for export shipment from the Gulf.

position day
According to the Chicago Board of Trade rules, the first day in the process of making or taking delivery of the actual commodity on a futures contract. The clearing firm representing the seller notifies the Board of Trade Clearing Corporation that its short customers want to deliver on a futures contract.

position limit (US)
The maximum number of futures (or options) contracts one can hold as determined by the Commodity Futures Trading Commission and/or the exchange upon which the contract is traded. Also referred to as *trading limit*.

position trader
Someone who takes long or short positions in futures markets in consequence of an opinion that prices are about to advance or decline and holds them for an extended period of time.

positive cashflow collar
A collar that is not a zero-cost collar.

positive yield curve
See **yield curve**.

PPS
Protected Payments System.

pre-allocation
The entry or assignment of a transaction into trade registration prior to its actual execution, anticipating that a trade will be effected at a later time.

pre-arrangement
The arrangement of a trade to be executed non-competitively in the pit. A pre-arranged trade represents a breach of the rules.

preference shares
Shares that normally pay a fixed rate of dividend as a per cent of the nominal value. Dividends and repayment are due to preference shareholders before ordinary shareholders, but after debenture and loan stock holders.

pre-market
See **inter-office**.

premium[1]
The excess of one futures contract price over that of another, or over the cash market price.

premium[2]
The amount a price would be increased to purchase a better quality commodity.

premium[3]
A futures delivery month selling at a higher price than another, as in 'July is at a premium over May'. See **contango** and **backwardation**.

premium[4]
Cash prices that are above the future, such as in foreign exchange. If the forward rate for Italian lira is at a premium to spot lira, it is selling above the spot price.

premium[5]
The money the buyer pays to the writer for granting an option contract.

price conversion factor
See **conversion factor** and **price factor**.

price delta
See **implied delta**.

price factor
The relative value of an actual deliverable bond when the actual bond has the same yield as the notional bond trading at par (i.e. when the actual bond has a yield equal to the coupon on the notional bond). Price factors are established for all deliverable bonds for each futures contract, calculated off the relative prices for the first day of the delivery month. This value, when multiplied by the settlement price, provides the price for the principal invoice amount. When accrued interest is added, this forms the invoice amount.

price feed
The electronic stream of transaction data supplied by the exchange to commercial quote vendors for onward sale and transmission.

price limit
The maximum advance or decline from the previous day's settlement price permitted for a contract in one trading session by the rules of the exchange. See also **variable limit**.

price limit order
A customer order that specifies the price at which a trade can be executed.

price manipulation
Any planned operation, transaction or practice calculated to cause, or maintain, an artificial price.

price transparency
The process of price discovery and open availability to all interested parties not merely those with privileged access to the market.

pricing
Using an exchange price (or a formula based on the average of such prices over a period) as the basis for determining the purchase price of physical goods.

pricing guide
A summary usually published daily of option premiums based on the previous day's settlement prices.

pricing terms
See **back-pricing**.

prime rate
Interest rate charged by major banks to their most creditworthy customers. (US)

primary market
The market in which securities are first issued to investors. *See* secondary market.

principal^1
A market-maker or dealer who is committed to giving a price (rate) for a deal or trade which is readily available to be taken.

principal^2
A person who has the counterparty risk to a trade.

principal invoice amount (LIFFE)
The initial amount first calculated when calculating the invoice amount to a buyer for the delivery of a bond against a notional bond futures contract. It is the EDSP x price factor of each bond deliverable at delivery of LIFFE long term interest rate contracts on long bonds. The markets are often too casual in reference to this and the invoice amount. The latter includes accrued interest.

principal trade
A proprietary order originated from an exchange member's own in-house account. Also called a *house order*.

private client
A private/personal investor as opposed to a commercial/institutional client.

private circuit
Alternative definition for dedicated line.

private wire
Wires leased by various firms and news agencies for the transmission of information to branch offices and subscriber clients.

privileges
An early form of agricultural options, no longer traded. (US)

producer price index (PPI)
An index that shows the cost of resources needed to produce manufactured goods. It is usually produced monthly.

profit-sharing forward
See **participating forward**[2].

profit taking
The liquidation of profitable open positions on the market in order to release profit on account at the clearing house.

prompt date
In relation to a contract (other than an option), the business day on which payment for delivery of the contract is to be settled.

PRS
The price reporting system, whereby all current pit information is transferred to the floor price display boards which is then disseminated throughout the world.

PSE
See **Pacific Stock Exchange**.

Pta
Textual abbreviation for Spanish peseta(s).

public elevators
Grain elevators in which bulk storage of grain is provided for the public for a fee.

pulpit
A raised structure adjacent to, or in the centre of, the pit or ring at a futures exchange where market reporters, employed by the exchange, record price changes as they occur in the trading pit.

purchasing hedge (or, long hedge)
Buying futures contracts to protect against a possible price increase of cash commodities that will be purchased in the future. At the time cash commodities are bought, the open futures position is closed by selling an equal number and type of futures contracts as those that were initially purchased. Also referred to as a *buying hedge*. See **hedging**.

put-call parity theorem
A description of the relationship between calls and puts with the same expiry date and exercise price derived from the fact that a long call option can be synthetically reproduced by a long put and long asset. It states that, for European options with the same exercise price, the cost of a call = cost of a put option + current underlying asset price - exercise price discounted to the current time. This relationship does not hold exactly for American-style options, and adjustments should be built in for any cashflows received from the underlying financial asset or storage costs if an underlying commodity.

put on (sterling deposits)
When a principal 'puts a broker on', the broker is given an order to arrange a deal on the principal's behalf. The broker may be put on either 'firm' or 'under reference', with or without a specified amount, or time limit. (*Bank of England Grey Book*).

put option
An option that gives the holder the right (but not the obligation), in exchange for payment of a premium, to sell the underlying asset at a specific price, and obligates the seller to buy the underlying asset at this specific price should the option be exercised. If the contract is an option on futures, the holder will obtain a short futures position if exercise takes place and the writer a long futures position, both at the exercise price.

put ratio backspread (options)
This position is the opposite to that of a put ratio spread. It is a bull call spread with a further purchased call at the lower exercise price, or a long straddle with lower cost traded off against reduced profits from an upwards movement. It is normally taken on when the market stands near the lower exercise price and is likely to become less volatile or move downwards. It is formed from long puts at the low exercise price with a short call at the higher exercise price, resulting in an expiry profile of a falling line to the lower exercise price, and then a rising line, to the higher exercise price, and then a flat line, plotted against the underlying asset. It may also be constructed synthetically using two short puts at the lower exercise price, a short call at the higher price, and a long underlying asset. Upside profit is

limited to the net premium income whilst profit potential if the market falls is open ended. Losses are incurred if the underlying asset stays at the lower exercise price. Time decay is greatest and works against the holder here, but is in the holder's favour if the underlying asset is above the higher exercise price.

put ratio spread (options)
The put ratio spread is a bear call spread with a further sold put at the lower exercise price, or a cheaper short straddle with upside risk reduced. It is a trade on the precision of pricing. It thus forms a profile of a rising line to the first exercise price, a falling line to the higher exercise price, and then a flat line thereafter, as the underlying asset price rises. It is used when the underlying asset market is near the higher exercise price and a slight fall is expected, but not a sharp price fall because unlimited losses could then be incurred. The selling of the additional put compared with the bear spread results in a low-cost strategy in exchange for this extra risk. More than two puts may be shorted to reduce cost further, but seldom more than three sold because of the downside risk. It is important to realize that the position is net short of puts. The position may also be constructed from a long call at the higher exercise price, short puts at the lower price, and a short underlying asset. All constructions are done to initial delta neutrality. Loss is limited to the net cost of the position if the underlying rises if constructed from puts, but is open-ended if the underlying falls, in proportion to the number of short positions. Time decay works in the holder's favour at the lower exercise price, and against the holder at the higher price.

put spread
A purchased put where the purchase cost is offset by the sale of another put at a lower exercise price. This results in a long bear spread. Advantageous if a market fall is expected.

put table top
Similar to a put ratio spread except that the short put options are at two different exercise prices. The expiry profile is thus rising from loss to profit, flat in profit, descending to around break-even, and then flat.

putting a price on (sterling deposits)
When a broker approaches a principal to 'put a price on' a transaction, then that price is for immediate acceptance or acceptance within an agreed period in respect of the particular transaction only - it does not amount to 'putting the broker on firm' for other transactions in or near to the particular period. (*Bank of England Grey Book* - Sterling Deposits).

put through
This is where a principal is prepared to take funds and on-lend them to a borrower to whom the original giver is, for whatever reason, not prepared to lend.

pyramiding
The use of profits on existing futures positions as margin to increase the size of the position, normally in successively smaller increments.

Q

qualified trader
An individual registered by an exchange as qualified to trade on the floor or on an automated trading system.

quotation
The current price available on the market at which purchases or sales may be executed.

quote vendor
An independent firm or organization who pays a fee to an exchange in return for access to the exchange's price feed. The price information is then reformatted and distributed publicly to subscribing clients of the quote vendor firm.

R

R^2
See **correlation coefficient**.

RAES
Retail Automated Execution System. The electronic trade execution system geared for retail orders on CBOT.

rainbow options
Options that offer the best performance of two or more selected markets, such as a call option on the greatest appreciation of the FT-All share or S&P 500. Also called an *outperformance option*.

rally
An upward movement of prices following a decline. Also known as a *recovery*.

random walk
A theory that price movements in the futures and securities markets are random in character.

range (price)
The price span during a given trading session, day, week, month, year, etc.

range forward
A fence or cylinder. See **bull cylinder** and **bear cylinder**.

ratio hedging
In financial futures trading, ratio hedging' usually refers to the calculation of the proper ratio of futures to cash. For example, considering ratio hedging in its most elementary form, the proper ratio for hedging $1 million of 13-7/8% T-bonds might be 14 T-bond futures contracts. This is because the futures contract is based on a contract unit with a coupon rate of 8%. The market value of the 13-7/8% T-bonds would be expected to more closely approximate the market value of fourteen futures contracts than it would ten futures contracts. This contract number is established using the price factor. See price factor and long-term interest rate contract.

ratio spreads
Spreads where the purchase of an in-the-money option is financed by the

sale of a greater number of out-of-the-money options. Ratio spreads can cause difficulties if the underlying asset subsequently becomes too volatile, changing the delta of the options to increase the value of the written positions. *See* call ratio spread and put ratio spread, call ratio backspread and put ratio backspread.

RCH
See **Recognized Clearing House.**

recaps
The process of reconciling orders executed against the various orders placed and details generated through trade matching and registration.

Recognized Clearing House
A UK clearing house recognized under the Financial Services Act. The LCH has this status.

Recognized Investment Exchange
A UK investment exchange that meets SIB requirements for recognition. These requirements include adequate financial resources, proper conduct of business rules, a proper and reasonably liquid market in its products, procedures for recording transactions, effective monitoring and enforcement of rules, and proper arrangements for clearing and performance of contracts. The LSE, LIFFE, IPE, LCE, LME and OMLX all have this status.

recovery
An upward movement of prices after a decline.

rectangle
A chart reversal pattern that is essentially an extended double or triple top or bottom.

redemption value
The value at which a financial instrument is redeemed. For bonds, this is the par value or nominal value, usually 100. Thus a 5-year, 10% coupon bond will pay a 10% coupon for 5 years, and the holder will then receive the redemption value of 100 as well.

registered commodity representative (RCR)
A broker, or customer's man. (US)

registered floor trader
A person who has passed the relevant examination process of a futures and

options exchange and may trade contracts on the floor of the exchange. They may trade but not give investment advice.

registered trader
A person who has passed the trader's examination process of an exchange and is allowed to deal on the exchange's markets for his or her firm.

registration[1]
The formal procedure of staff registration at various levels of authorization and accountability with an exchange's membership and operations departments.

registration[2]
The official handshake between an exchange and its clearing house to the effect that a transaction has been properly executed, matched and is eligible for registration for the purposes of securing the clearing house's guarantee as to performance.

registered trade
A transaction that has been matched and passed to the clearing house for guarantee.

regular-way settlement (currency asset markets)
Trades in which the settlement occurs the next business day after the trade date.

regulated commodities
Commodities traded on futures exchanges that were subject to Commodity Exchange Authority regulation prior to the Commodity Futures Trading Commission Act of 1974. Presently, any commodity traded on contract markets for future delivery.

relative strength indicator (RSI)
A charting measure that indicates a market is overbought or oversold.

renouncable documents
These are documents that provide temporary evidence of ownership of equities and are in bearer form. They are thus valuable. An allotment letter notifies successful applicants for a company share offer that they have received stock; a provisional allotment letter notifies shareholders of a rights issue; a renouncable certificate informs shareholders of a capitalization issue. Each document includes full instruction on what holders may do if

they wish to register the shares in their own name or transfer them to someone else.

reporting level or limit
Sizes of positions set by the exchanges or the CFTC at or above which commodity traders and brokers who carry their account must make daily reports as to the size of the position by commodity, delivery month, and whether the position is speculative or hedging.

repurchase agreements (or, repo)
An agreement between a seller and a buyer, usually in US government securities, in which the seller agrees to buy back the security at a later date.

reserve requirements
The minimum amount of cash and liquid assets as a percentage of demand deposits and time deposits that member banks of the Federal Reserve are required to maintain.

resistance
A level above which prices have had difficulty penetrating. Used in technical analysis.

resistance line
A trendline drawn through peaks in a falling market. Used in technical analysis.

resting order
See **limit order**.

restricted life option
An equity option formerly listed on LTOM with a 3- and 6-month expiry cycle. LTOM contracts were normally 3, 6 and 9 months. Now de-listed by LIFFE.

resumption
The re-opening, on the following day, of specific futures and options markets that also trade during the evening session at the Chicago Board of Trade.

retail price index (RPI)
An index that measures the change in prices of a fixed basket of goods and services purchased retail. The UK RPI surveys about 600 items and is compiled monthly. Because it is independently produced and not subject to re-

vision, it forms the reference for coupons and redemption payments on index-linked gilts. *See also* **consumer price index**.

retender
In specific circumstances, some contract markets permit holder of futures contracts who have received a delivery notice through the clearing house to sell a futures contract and return the notice to the clearing house for re-issue to another long; others permit transfer of notices to another buyer.

retractable
A feature that gives investors the right to sell a bond back to the issuer prior to a stated maturity achieving the same function as an investor put.

return line
A line on a price chart drawn through a series of ascending peaks in a bull market, or declining troughs in a bear market. It is used with trendlines to form trend channels.

revaluation
A formal official' increase in the exchange rate of a currency. *See* **devaluation**.

reversal
See **option reversal**.

reversal day
A technical analysis term used to indicate that a new high in an uptrend is followed by a lower close on the same day (*topping reversal day*) or a new low in a downtrend is followed by a higher close on the same day (Bottom reversal day). In each case, a signal that the existing trend will reverse. *See* key day reversal, island reversal and two-day reversal.

reversal pattern
A chart pattern that indicates that the existing price trend has finished and will be reversed.

revolving facilities
Loan facilities that are drawndown, in part or in whole, and then repaid again in part or in whole, and subsequently redrawn. This process can be repeated as often as the documentation permits.

RFC
Registered floor clerk.

RFT
Registered floor trader. A person registered to trade on an exchange floor.

rho
A measure of the sensitivity of options positions to interest rates. This will impact upon the future price of the option and the time value of the premium.

riding the yield curve
Trading in interest rate futures according to the expectations of a change in the yield curve. Also similarly trading in bonds.

RIE
See **Recognized Investment Exchange**.

rights issue
An offer of new shares made to existing shareholders in proportion to their current holdings. The quoting of the proportion has different meanings in the UK and in the US. Normally the rights issue is offered at a discount to the current market price.

ring[1]
Space on trading floor where futures are traded. Also known as a *pit*.

ring[2] (LME)
An exchange open-outcry trading session in a metal, of such duration and at such times as are laid down by the London Metal Exchange.

risk
The chance of an outcome not occurring as planned. This may be due to an actual return differing from a previously predicted return. The variability of such predicted returns can be estimated using statistical tools such as standard deviations and probability distributions. In addition risk may arise from interest rate or foreign exchange rate changes, counterparty failure, issuer default and many other causes.

risk disclosure statement
A document enumerating some of the risks involved in trading futures and/or options that a client must sign before opening an account with a brokerage firm.

risk factors
A measurement of an option position or premium in relation to the underlying instrument. *See also* **delta**.

risk management
The practice of continuously assessing and controlling all known exposures and hedging such risks to a sustainable level or where applicable maximizing profitable returns.

RLO
Restricted life option. A short maturity equity option formerly traded on LTOM, but since de-listed by LIFFE.

rolling settlement
Settlement that occurs a specified number of calendar or business days after the trade date.

Roll option pricing model
A model that prices American-style equity call options.

roll-over
A special trading procedure involving the shift of one month of a spread into another future month, while holding the other contract month. The shift can take place in either the long or short month. The term also applies to lifting a near futures position and re-establishing it in a more deferred delivery month. Also the movement of a position held in one trading month of a contract by trading out of it and trading into the same position in a further dated month.

roll-overs (sterling deposits)
A 'roll-over' loan is a loan for a fixed period during which there are regular specified intervals at which the interest rate is re-established. A 'roll-over' or 're-issuable' CD is one on which the term—but not always the rate of interest—is fixed, but a new CD is issued at specific intervals.

Room (The) (LME)
Literally the room where open-outcry trading takes place on the London Metal Exchange, both in the ring and by kerb trading outside the ring.

ROT
Registered options trader.

rotated cylinder (options)
A bull cylinder with an expiry profile rotated clockwise 45° or a bear cylinder rotated anticlockwise 45° giving profiles that appear like a short synthetic future with a split strike, or a long synthetic future with a split strike, respectively. Both strategies must involve the use of the underlying asset. *See also* **bear rotated cylinder** and **bull rotated cylinder**.

rotation
The formal opening procedure to commence dealing in an option contract.

round trip/turn
The term used to describe a completed transaction from the opening of a position to the subsequent liquidating/closing sale or purchase, against which a dealing or transaction fee (net of any actual transaction profit or loss) is levied.

RPB
Recognized Professional Body. (UK)

RPI
See **retail price index**.

RSI
See **relative strength indicator**.

runaway gap
See **measuring gap**.

runners
Messengers who rush orders received by phone clerks to brokers for execution in the pit.

run through
The opening or closing call-over of quotations to establish prices on commodity markets.

S

SAEF
The London Stock Exchange SEAQ Automated Execution Facility. It enables small trades in UK shares to be executed automatically with a market-maker through a computer terminal instead of over the telephone.

SAFE[1]
Simulation Analysis of Financial Exposure. (CBOT)

SAFE[2]
Synthetic Agreement for Forward Exchange.

SAFEX
See **South African Futures Exchange**.

São Paulo Stock Exchange Bovespa Index
Equity index on the Brazilian Stock Exchange.

scale down (or up)
To purchase or sell on scale down means to buy or sell at regular price intervals in a declining market. To buy or sell on scale up means to buy or sell at regular price intervals as the market advances.

scale order
This type of order is a market or limit order which instructs the broker to buy or sell additional contracts at different price levels after the original fill. If a client thought the market was rising he or she might instruct a broker to buy it at a price, and to buy another 5 contracts every time the price fell, say, a further 10 ticks.

scalper
One who trades for small gains. This trader normally establishes and liquidates a position quickly, usually within the same day.

Sch
Textual abbreviation for Austrian schilling(s).

scratch trade
A facility offered to locals (individual market traders) whereby they are al-

lowed to net off, on an intra-day basis, all trades with a common sale and purchase price without incurring any exchange transaction charge. It is a legitimate practice designed to improve market/contract liquidity.

scrip issue
See **capitalization issue.**

SDA
Stanza Delivery Agent. *See* **Stanza di Compensazione Titoli.**

SDR
Special Drawing Right. This is a basket currency like the Ecu but used as an accounting currency by the IMF and World Bank etc.

SEAQ
Stock Exchange Automated Quotation System of the London Stock Exchange. It is a continuously updated price display system showing market-maker quotes, trade publication, company news and other announcements. Prices shown are confirmed by telephone and dealt over the telephone.

SEAQ International
The London Stock Exchange price quotation system for its International Equity market. It is similar to SEAQ.

secondary market
The market in which securities that have already been issued trade between market-makers, dealers, investors, etc. *See* **primary market.**

second currency options
These pay out in a currency different to that of the underlying asset, based on a notional principal amount. For example the percentage performance of the CAC-40 payable in sterling, based on a notional amount of pounds.

second month
The second shortest maturity contract trading at the current time.

securities
Financial instruments such as bonds, shares, bills, CDs, etc.

Securities and Investments Board (SIB)
The body which oversees the UK financial services industry.

security deposit - initial
A cash amount of funds that must be deposited with the broker for each contract as a guarantee of fulfilment of the futures contract. It is not considered as part payment or purchase.

segregated customer
Any customer whose money is segregated from the firm s under the Financial Services (Client's Money) Regulations 1987.

SEK
Standard foreign exchange code for Swedish krona (kronor).

seller
A trader originating an offer or accepting a counterparty bid.

seller in
The trader currently offering best market price or accepting market bids at the end of a call-over period. The trader may then claim priority for later buy orders. It only may apply in markets that operate a call-over system.

seller over
An offerer who is still offering at the same price after having fulfilled only part of his or her order at that price at the end of a call-over period. The offerer may then claim priority status. It only may apply in markets that operate a call-over system. *See* **buyer over**.

seller's call
Same as the buyer's call except that the seller has the right to determine the time to fix the price.

selling basis
Term meaning that the buying basis is increased to include costs and profits.

selling hedge (or short hedge)
Selling futures contracts to protect against possible declining prices of financial instruments or commodities that will be sold in the future. At the time the cash, financial instruments or commodities are sold, the open futures position is closed by purchasing an equal number and type of futures contracts as those that were initially sold. *See also* **hedge ratio (futures)**.

semi-fabricator
A producer of semis (semi-finished products).

semis
Metal which has been fashioned into any of a number of recognized shapes such as tube, angle, etc.

SEPON
Stock Exchange Pool Nominees. A part of the TALISMAN settlement system of the London Stock Exchange.

series
All options of the same class and with the same exercise price and expiry date form a series.

Service Company
Under the Financial Services Act, a company providing a strategic market service but who is regulated by the SIB directly as opposed to an SRO.

settlement business day
A business day on which commercial banks are open in New York City, for the settlement of international transactions in US dollars.

settlement price
The official price for a financial or commodity derivative at which all open positions on an exchange are revalued for the purposes of profit and loss and subsequent margin calculation at the end of each business day. The settlement price is a calculated value that takes into consideration the closing offer and bid price, the last actual traded price and a weighted average of prices traded during the last few minutes of the close of trading.

settlement price (LME)
The official cash seller's price at the close of the second ring of official trading. Is used as the basis for trades in physical metal done outside the LME, as well as for internal accounting purposes on all LME trades now prompt for settlement.

SFA
Securities and Futures Authority, the UK self-regulatory organization for these areas of the financial industry.

SFE
See **Sydney Futures Exchange**.

SFr
Textual abbreviation for Swiss franc(s).

short[1]
One who has sold a futures contract to establish a market position and who has not yet closed out the position through an offsetting purchase. The opposite of long. Holding more contracts to sell than to buy, or to sell than underlying instruments held.

short[2]
A short maturity instrument or contract, i.e. short gilts meaning gilts with less than seven years to maturity.

short add-on
An additional amount of margin call added to settlement values and applied to the writers or sellers of short options positions.

short basis
See **short the basis**.

short bear spread
See **bear spread**.

short bull spread
See **bull spread**.

short butterfly (options)
This strategy is composed of a large number of options positions and carries the danger that commission costs can negate profits. It is named a short position, although its profile is more akin to the long profiles of a straddle or strangle. It is referred to as a short position because the maximum gain is net premium income. It is comprised of a short call at exercise price E_1, two long calls at E_2, and a short call at E_3 where $E_3 > E_2 > E_1$ and $E_3 - E_2 = E_2 - E_1$. Alternatively, construct from a short put at E_1, two long puts at E_2 and a short put at E_3. Other versions are a short put at E_1, long put at E_2, long call at E_2 and short call at E_3, or, a short call at E_1, long call at E_2, long put at E_2 and short put at E_3. It is a position taken on when the underlying asset is below E_1 or above E_3 and the position is overpriced with a month or thereabouts left. Alternatively, it may be sold when only a few weeks are left, the market is near E_2 and an imminent move is expected in either direction. The expiry profile is a flat profit to E_1, downward to E_2, rising to E_3 and a flat gain above that. The maximum loss occurs if the market remains at or around E_2 at expiry. Time decay is negligible until the final month, moving fastest when the underlying asset is priced around E_2.

short call option
A strategy to be used only when there is a firm conviction that the market is not going up. If only partly convinced, a better strategy is to sell out-of-the-money (higher exercise price) options. If very confident that the market will stagnate or fall, at-the-money calls should be sold. If it is not thought that the market will stagnate, in-the-money options should be sold. With this short position, the maximum profit is the premium received. This is obtained if the underlying does not rise above the exercise price. If the underlying does go above the exercise price then losses can be unlimited, and hence the position must be closely monitored. Volatility increases work against the seller, but time value decay is in the short position holder's favour. The position may be created synthetically from a short underlying asset and a short put. The expiry profile is a flat line representing premium income up to the exercise price and then a declining 45° line. *See also* **covered call option**.

short condor (options)
A strategy comparable to a short butterfly from which it differs in having four different exercise prices instead of three. The centre section is thus flat instead of a downward point. The expiry profile is thus flat, descending, flat, ascending, flat.

short covering
Buying to offset an existing short position.

short futures position
A sold future, based on an expectation of a falling market, profits can be taken if the futures market falls. Profits and losses are based on the difference between the sale price and the subsequent purchase price. There is no exposure to volatility or time decay. The position may be synthetically reproduced from a short call and a long put at the same exercise price. The profile is a 45° downward sloping line.

short hedge
The sale of futures contracts to eliminate, or lessen, the possible decline in value of ownership of an approximately equal amount of the actual physical commodity or financial instrument. *See* **selling hedge**.

short-instrument conversion
See **option reversal**.

short option box
See **option box**.

short (over-sold)
Excess of sales over purchases.

short put option
A strategy that can be employed if it is firmly believed that the market is not going down. If very confident that the underlying asset will stagnate or rise, at-the-money options should be sold. If only partly convinced, out-of-the-money (lower exercise price) options should be sold. If in doubt about market stagnation, then in-the-money options should be sold. Profits are limited to premium income if the underlying rises, but losses can be as much as the full amount of the exercise price if the asset falls in price. Increased volatility will work against the position but time decay is advantageous. The position can be created synthetically from a long underlying asset and a short call option. The expiry profile is a line rising at 45° from a loss area to equal the premium income as the underlying asset reaches the exercise price. If the market falls, the holder will be exercised against and required to purchase the asset. Thereafter as the asset rises the profile is a flat line representing premium income as the asset rises and no exercise takes place.

short rotated cylinder (options)
See **bear rotated cylinder**.

short selling
Selling a contract or option with the idea of delivering or of buying to offset it at a later date. This is uncovered selling.

short squeeze
A situation in which the lack of supplies tends to force persons who had gone short to cover their positions by offset at higher prices.

short straddle (options)
A strategy to be employed when the underlying market is priced near the common exercise price of the strategy's component options, a market stagnation is expected, and a decline in volatility is foreseen. However, losses are open if a significant movement takes place. The position is constructed from a short put and a short call at the same exercise price. It may also be constructed from two short calls and a long underlying asset, or two short puts and a short asset. The expiry profile shows open-ended losses in either direction, depicted by downward lines from the initial point of combined premium income. As with the long straddle, it is normally established to delta neutrality. The position must be closely monitored and readjusted to delta neutrality if the market moves away from the exercise price. Profits

from time-value decay accumulate at an increasing rate as expiry approaches.

short strangle (options)
A less risky version of a short straddle, it may be used when the underlying asset lies within the range of the two exercise prices involved and though active, is becoming less volatile. If this occurs, the holder profits, if it remains active then there is less risk involved than with a straddle. The position is formed from a short put and a short call, at exercise price E_1 and E_2. The put or call options may be assigned to either exercise price where $E_2 > E_1$. (If both options are out-of-the-money the position may be referred to as a *combination* or, if in-the-money, as a *guts*. There is thus conflict over terminology of which definition is a pure strangle). The expiry profile is a line upwards to the lower exercise price, flat between the exercise prices at a gain of combined premium cost, and then a downward sloping line. Alternatively, it may be constructed by reproducing synthetically one of the options positions. It should be set up to initial delta neutrality. Maximum profits are obtained if the market stays between the two exercise prices and equals the premium income if constructed of calls and puts only. At expiry losses are made only if the market is below E_1, or above E_2, by the amount of the premium income. Loss potential is open-ended as many traders holding this position in IBM in April 1978 found to their cost—this resulting in the name 'strangle' being applied to the strategy. Increases in volatility work against the holder, time decay in the holder's favour, picking up at an increasing rate as expiry approaches. This strategy may be employed by fund managers who think that a stock they hold would be overvalued at the high exercise price and undervalued at the low exercise price. If the price rises they are happy to be exercised against and sell the overvalued stock. If the price falls then it might be regarded as cheap and the fund manager will happily add it to his or her portfolio if exercised against. The main danger is if the stock collapses.

short synthetic asset
A short cash position created synthetically with a long put option and a short call option at the same exercise price.

short synthetic futures (split strike)
Can also be a zero-cost option. The strategy offers a bearish view, as with a short future, but is constructed with options and has a central area of limited gain or loss. It is constructed from a long put at one exercise price and a short call at a higher exercise price, the long premium cost and short premium income virtually offsetting each other. Profit increases as the market for the underlying falls below the put exercise price, and losses are in-

curred if the underlying rises above the short call exercise price. Time decay works against the holder if futures are lower, or in the holder's favour if futures are higher. The profit is a downward sloping line, then flat between the two exercise prices, then sloping down again. *See also* **rotated cylinder**.

short-term interest rate contract
A contract on a notional 3-month euro-deposit to be made at the expiry/delivery of the contract. No deposit is actually made. At expiry, all open positions are closed out and profits/losses on the contract obtained through variation margin payments. The seller of futures is selling the underlying deposit, that is, acting like a bank, while a buyer buys the deposit, that is, acting like a depositor. The quote system employed is 100 minus the reference interest rate. In this way, if rates rise, then the futures price falls. An inverse relationship between price and rate is therefore imposed, making the instrument comparable in response to yields to a bond or money market instrument. Options on these exchange-traded 3-month interest rate contracts are usually options on futures. The buyer of a call would be expecting to see interest rates fall.

short Texas 'hedge' (options)
A short underlying position geared up with the addition of a long put. This is a speculative position and shows very geared profits if the underlying falls.

short the basis
A person or firm who has sold the spot commodity short and hedged with a purchase of futures is said to be short the basis. If basis increases the position may make money, if it decreases it will lose money. *See also* **long the basis**.

SIB
See **Securities and Investments Board**.

sigma
Same as **vega**.

SIMEX
See **Singapore International Financial Futures Exchange Ltd**.

Simulation Analysis of Financial Exposure (SAFE)
A sophisticated computer risk-analysis program that monitors the risk of clearing members and large-volume traders at the Chicago Board of Trade.

It calculates the risk of change in market prices or volatility to a firm carrying open positions.

Singapore International Financial Futures Exchange Ltd. (SIMEX)
A Far East exchange which lists futures and options on currencies, interest rates, indices and oil.

SIR
Standard Indonesian Rubber. SIR 20 has traded on London Fox.

skip day settlement (currency asset markets)
Settlement on the second business day following the trade date. Usage of this term is confined to the US domestic market; known as *spot settlement* in the UK foreign exchange markets.

SKr
Textual abbreviation for Swedish krona (kronor).

small traders
Traders who are not required to file reports of their futures transactions or position. Their combined positions are derived by subtracting large traders' commitments from the total open interest. Accordingly, the number of small traders is unknown.

SOFFEX
See **Swiss Options and Financial Futures Exchange**.

soft
A weak market.

Soft Red Winter
A type of low protein soft wheat.

softs
A general term describing those commodities (in relation to futures markets) that are not metals, such as cocoa, wheat, sugar, etc.

sold-out-market
When liquidation has been completed and offerings become scarce, the market is said to be sold out.

South African Futures Exchange (SAFE)
Located in Johannesburg, it lists contracts on gold, bonds, interest rates and equity indices.

S&P 100, 500
Standard and Poor's US equity indexes based on 100 stocks and 500 stocks, respectively.

SPAN
Standard Portfolio Analysis of Margin. The system used for assessing margin levels on exchanges in the UK and US, originally introduced by the CME. The London Clearing House version is referred to as *London Span*.

specialist (US)
A market-maker granted exclusive rights by an exchange to make a market in a specific underlying. In return for making a fair and orderly market, such persons may both trade on their own account and act as a broker for exchange members.

specialist market-maker
Same as a designated market-maker, except that a specialist will normally enjoy contract exclusivity.

speculator
A market participant who tries to profit from buying and selling futures and options contracts by anticipating future price movements. Speculators assume market price risk and add liquidity and capital to the futures markets.

speed
A measure of the change in gamma in relation to a change in the underlying asset price.

spike top
A chart pattern showing a very fast market move that is beyond expectations. Prices reverse trend quickly and without warning.

split execution
A transaction that involved more than one counterparty in order to fulfil the contract volume.

split strike (options)
See **long synthetic future** and **short synthetic future**.

spot[1]
Usually refers to a cash market price for a financial instrument or physical commodity that is available for immediate delivery.

spot[2]
Term denoting immediate delivery for cash as distinct from future delivery.

spot commodity
The actual commodity as distinguished from futures. Same as actuals or cash commodity.

spot month
The first month in which delivery can take place and for which a quotation is made on the futures market. *See also* **first month, front month, second month.**

spot price
The price at which a physical commodity is selling at a given time and place. Same as **cash price.**

spot settlement (foreign exchange and currency deposit markets)
Cash settlement two working days from the current date.

spread (futures)
Refers to a simultaneous purchase and sale of futures contracts for the same commodity or financial instrument for delivery in different months or in different but related markets. *See* **inter-market spread** and **intra-market spread.**

spread (options)
The purchase and sale of different series of options by the same principal. *See* **vertical spread** and **horizontal spread.**

spreading
The simultaneous purchase and sale of two related markets in the expectation that a profit will be obtained when the position is offset. Examples include buying one futures contract and selling another futures contract of the same underlying asset but different delivery month; buying and selling the same delivery month of the same asset on different futures exchanges; buying a given delivery month of one futures market and selling the same delivery month of a different, but related, futures market. *See* **spread.**

spread margin
The margin required for a spread. Because a spread reduces risk, the margin requirement may be lower than for each contract involved separately.

spread order
This is an order to buy and sell two different delivery months in one contract or two different contracts themselves. The actual order is given at a differential rate between the two sides of the spread. The order can be based on an intra-market spread and executed on a differential basis between the futures prices.

SQQ
Standard Quality Quotation price of the Meat and Livestock Commission. (UK)

square
A situation in which purchases and sales are equal.

squeeze
Situation in which those who are short cannot repurchase their contracts, except at a price substantially higher than the value of those contracts in relation to the rest of the market.

SRO
Self Regulatory Organization. A body established under UK Financial Services Act, 1986.

stag
A person who applies for a new issue of shares in the hope that it will rise in price as soon as dealing starts, whereupon the holding is liquidated for an immediate profit.

stamp duty
A UK tax levied on the purchaser of shares at a percentage of the purchase price.

standard market terminology
The trading language used on the market floor.

standard order form
The order form used as an official receipt of all in-coming orders onto the market floor. These forms must be immediately completed and time-stamped before communication to the trading pit for execution.

Stanza di Compensazione Titole
The settlement agency in Italy through which delivery of LIFFE BTP contracts is made.

steer/corn ratio
The relationship of cattle prices to feeding costs. It is measured by dividing the price of cattle ($/hundredweight) by the price of corn ($/bushel). When corn prices are high relative to cattle prices, fewer units of corn equal the dollar value of 100 pounds of cattle. Conversely, when corn prices are low in relation to cattle prices, more units of corn are required to equal the value of 100 pounds of beef. *See* **feed ratio**.

stock index
An indicator used to measure and report value changes in a selected group of stocks. How a particular stock index tracks the market depends on its composition, the sampling of stocks, the weighting of individual stocks, and the method of averaging used to establish an index.

stock index future
A future on a stock index such as the FTSE 100 Index (UK), Standard and Poor's 500 (S&P 500) (US), etc. The futures trade the index at a fixed sum per point. The FTSE 100 Index contract is valued at £25 a point and the S&P 500 contract at $500 a point. All stock index futures are cash-settled at delivery. The same principles apply to metal and shipping price indices. *See also* index contract.

stock type settlement
Settlement procedure where the purchase of a contract demands full and immediate payment to the seller. In addition, the actual cash gain or loss on a position is not realized until the position is liquidated.

stop levels
Price levels in a given contract at which orders have been placed for execution that either takes a predetermined profit or limits the amount of loss on a declining position.

stop order
An order to buy or sell that becomes a market order when the market reaches a specified price. A stop order to buy becomes a market order when the commodity or security trades (or is bid) at, or above, the stop price. A stop order to sell becomes a market order when the commodity or security trades (or is offered) at, or below, the stop price. A sell stop is placed below the market, a buy stop is placed above the market.

stop-limit order
A variation of a stop order in which a trade must be executed at the exact price or better. If the order cannot be executed, it is held until the stated price or better is reached again. It is feasible for the stop and limit price to be the same.

stop-loss order
A buying or selling order at a named price, and placed in advance, which can be fulfilled only when the market price has reached the level specified by the client. As soon as the price has been traded, the order is executed at the next obtainable price. There is no guarantee that the order will be executed at the level specified in the original order. Such an order is used as a safety net to get out of a position if the market moves in an opposite director to the holder's view.

straddle (futures)
The simultaneous purchase and sale of the same futures contract, or commodity on the same market, but for different delivery months.

straddle (options)
This is where an investor buys both a put and a call option or writes both a put and a call option on an underlying security at the same exercise prices. *See also* **long** and **short straddle**.

straddle calendar spread (options)
Sale of a straddle in a near month and purchase of a straddle in a far month at the same strike. A trade undertaken for the same reasons a time spread is put on, but also perhaps combining a volatility view in the trade. *See also* **diagonal straddle, calendar spread.**

straight (sterling deposit)
The words 'straight dates' mean 'even dates', i.e. a CD or deposit maturing on the same date of the month (e.g. 16 January - 16 July). Long sixes or short sixes are maturities either side of this date.

strangle
This is where an investor buys both a put and a call option, or writes both a put and a call option on an underlying security, at different exercise prices. *See also* **long strangle** and **short strangle**.

strap
An asymmetrical straddle. It comprises two long (short) calls and one long (short) put, with the same expiry and exercise price.

strike price
The price specified in an options contract. *See* **exercise price.**

strike rate
Same as strike price, but is the terminology used in currency options.

strip
An asymmetrical straddle. It comprises one long (short) call and two long (short) puts, with the same expiry and exercise price.

strong hands
When used in connection with delivery of commodities on futures contracts, the term usually means that the party receiving the delivery notice probably will take delivery and retain ownership of the commodity. When used in connection with futures positions, the term usually means positions held by trade interests or financial institutions.

subject
There are two common usages of 'subject'. *Subject bid (or offer):* Price subject to purchaser's approval of names which would be dependent on credit limits. *Bid (or offer) subject:* Indication of a price a purchaser is willing to pay but may not be firm. (As used in the *Bank of England Grey Book*).

support
The place on a chart where buying is sufficient to halt a price decline.

support line
A trendline drawn on a price chart through the troughs of an upward price movement in a market. It indicates the points where the market is finding support.

swap
A contractual agreement to exchange a stream of periodic payments with a counterparty. These may be fixed for floating interest rate commitments (*plain vanilla swap*), one currency for another (*currency swap*), both the above (*cocktail swap*), and there are many other varieties too, such as *basis swaps*, *receiver swaps* and *asset swaps*. *Swaptions*, or *options on swaps*, form a liquid area of the market.

swap (foreign exchange and currency deposit markets)
A spot sale against a forward purchase or spot purchase against a forward sale. When talking about 'forwards' dealers refer only to the forward date,

e.g. if a dealer buys spot and sells three months forward, he or she will say to a counterparty, "I offer threes" or "I sell threes".

swaption
An option on a swap.

SWIFT
The system of electronic bank transfers used in Europe.

SWINGS
Sterling warrants into gilt-edged securities.

Swiss Options and Financial Futures Exchange A.G. (SOFFEX)
Located in Zurich, it lists options on equity and equity indices, also three-month Swiss franc futures and Low Exercise Price Options (LEPOs).

switch
Offsetting a position in one delivery month of a financial instrument or commodity and simultaneous initiation of a similar position in another delivery month of the same commodity. When used by hedgers, this tactic is referred to as *rolling forward* the hedge. See **spread**.

SYCOM
Sydney Computerized Overnight Market, the after-hours dealing system of the SFE.

Sydney Futures Exchange (SFE)
An Australian exchange which lists contracts on cattle, wool, acceptances, Treasury bonds and the All-Ordinaries Share Price Index.

symmetrical triangle
A chart pattern that can be either a reversal or continuation pattern depending upon the length of time it lasts. If it lasts three to six months or more, it is a *reversal*; less than three months, a *continuation pattern*.

Synthetic Agreement for Forward Exchange (SAFE)
The generic term for exchange rate agreements (ERAs) and forward exchange agreements (FXAs), developed to overcome the capital adequacy problems of forex forwards highlighted by the Bank for International Settlements (BIS) capital adequacy regulations. These treat ERAs and FXAs as interest rate, rather than foreign exchange, instruments which means that for the purposes of the regulations, banks need provide less capital to support their obligations.

T

table top
A strategy comparable to a ratio spread except that the short options are at two different exercise prices. The eall ratio spread expiry profile is thus amended to be flat, ascending, flat, descending, and the put ratio spread a rising, flat, falling, flat expiry profile.

take-off (sterling deposits)
When a principal 'takes a broker off' either a single order or several orders, he or she must, if the broker has been put on 'firm', check whether the broker is already committed to deal on his or her behalf.

take-out
The additional cash to be received on the sale of one block of securities and purchase of another. *See* **pay-up**.

taker
The buyer of an option contract.

take the offer
Buy at the offer price.

TALISMAN
Transfer Account Lodgement for Investors, Stock Management for Market-Makers. The London Stock Exchange's computerized settlement system for equities.

TAURUS
The London Stock Exchange's share registration system that was to avoid the need for ownership of share certificates. These were to be replaced by monthly statements. The project was cancelled in early 1993.

T-bills, T-bonds
See **Treasury bills, US Treasury bonds**.

technical analysis
Anticipating future price movement using historical prices, trading volume, open interest and other trading data to study price patterns. The analysis is

based on three principal tenets: (I) That market prices discount all information, (2) that prices move in trends, and (3) that history repeats itself.

technical position
Term used to indicate internal market conditions. When the market is sold out or is oversold, its technical position is said to be strong. Conversely, after a sharp advance when a market is overbought, its technical position is said to be weak.

technical rally (or decline)
A price movement resulting from technical conditions developing within a market itself and not dependent on outside supply and demand factors.

TED spread
The spread obtained from US Treasury bond and eurodollar futures. This is a trade based on yield changes at different maturities and qualities.

telephone/phone broker
A trader who interfaces clients/back office dealers with the actual pit traders, so called because of the principle duties involving the relay of information to and from the exchange floor.

tender
The act of giving notice to the clearing house of intention to initiate delivery of the physical commodity in satisfaction of the futures contract. *See* **retender**.

tenderable grades and staples
These are grades and staples deliverable to settle a futures contract.

terminal elevator
An elevator located at a point of greatest accumulation in the movement of agricultural products which stores the commodity or moves it to the processors.

terminal market
Usually synonymous with commodity exchange or futures market, especially in the UK. Also used to signify principals' markets as opposed to brokers' market.

Texas 'hedge'
Long the underlying geared up with the addition of a long call, or short the

underlying together with a long put. The directional view is much more geared. It is not a hedge at all.

TFE/TSE
See **Toronto Futures Exchange/Toronto Stock Exchange.**

TGE
See **Tokyo Grain Exchange.**

the figure
An alternative term for **'double O'**.

theoretical edge
The price difference between the theoretical price of an option position or strategy and its market price. A positive theoretical edge shows the strategy is trading cheap if purchased, or expensive if sold. A negative theoretical edge is the opposite.

theoretical value
Option value generated by an option valuation model.

theta
The effect of change in time to expiration on theoretical values of calls and puts, the rate at which a long option loses its value as time passes, the daily cost of holding a long option or the amount of revenue received daily for holding a short position (depending upon how measured). It is either measured in money per day or as a per cent of price. It is usually given a positive value for long positions, but not everyone abides by this convention, so caution should taken! Theta is non-linear and greater for options close to expiration. The more the market and exercise prices diverge then the less effect theta has on an option's price. Negative theta is generally associated with negative gamma, and vice-versa.

three-month interest rate contract
See **short-term interest rate contract.**

tick
The smallest allowable increment of price movement for a contract. Also referred to as *minimum price fluctuation*.

tick chart
A price chart that charts futures or options trades.

ticker tape
A continuous paper tape transmission of commodity or security prices, volume and other trading information which operates on private leased wires by the exchanges, available to their member firms and other interested parties on a subscription basis.

tidying-up period (IPE and LME)
Refers to the 2-minute clearing up process on the futures contracts.

TIFFE
See **Tokyo International Financial Futures Exchange**.

time and sales
The bids, offers, traded prices, time and estimated volume as observed by an exchange pit observer and then recorded in the sequence in which they occurred.

time decay
The loss of value in a long option position due to the passage of time and the reduced potential for profitable exercise. Decay is non-linear, moving at a faster pace closer to expiry. It is measured mathematically by theta. For a long position, time decay works against the holder, for a short position it works in the holder's favour.

time or time limit order
A customer order that designates the time during which it can be executed. In addition to giving the actual time, a time order may be used to denote the life of an open order.

time spread
An options strategy designed to profit from the fact that option prices do not show a linear decline in time value. Time value falls faster near to expiry. Thus the strategy shorts a near contract and goes long on an equivalent longer maturity contract. So, a 3-month call exercise at 100 exercise price may be sold, and covered by a 6-month long call with the same exercise price. Three months later, the short call will have expired and the original 6-month long position may be closed. The profit on the expired call will be reduced by the loss on the long position. If the call were exercised against the holder, the long position will provide cover. Alternatively, a 6-month call could be shorted, covered by a long 9-month call etc. A holder of a time spread wants the market to sit still and profit from the faster rate of time decay on the short option than the long option.

time stamp
The time-logging machine which records the exact time an order is received and when it is executed.

time value
The amount of money option buyers are willing to pay for an option in the anticipation that, over time, a change in the underlying price will cause the option to increase in value. In general, an option premium is the sum of time value and intrinsic value. Any amount by which an option premium exceeds the option's intrinsic value can be considered time value. Also referred to as *extrinsic value*. If an option premium is 20, and intrinsic value is 12, time value is 8. If intrinsic value is 0, time value is 20.

TIMS
Theoretical Indicative Margin System, a system that has been used by some US exchanges for margining options as an alternative to SPAN.

TOCOM
See **Tokyo Commodity Exchange**.

Tokyo Commodity Exchange (TOCOM)
A Japanese exchange which lists contracts on cotton, rubber, wool and precious metals.

Tokyo Grain Exchange (TGE)
A Japanese exchange which lists contracts on corn, redbeans and soybeans.

Tokyo International Financial Futures Exchange (TIFFE)
A Japanese exchange which lists contracts on currencies and interest rates.

Tokyo Stock Exchange (TSE)
A Japanese exchange which lists contracts on Japanese government bonds, US T-bonds and the TOPIX stock index.

tone
Any of a number of adjectives used to describe the general state and movement of a commodity market. For example a rising market might be described as firm or strong; a declining market, weak; a flat or low volatility market might be steady or about steady, etc.

TOPIC
The London Stock Exchange's own videotext terminal network that is used

to disseminate SEAQ and SEAQ International, as well as other market information.

TOPIX
Tokyo Stock Price Index.

topping reversal day
A technical analysis term used to indicate that a new high in an uptrend is followed by a lower close on the same day, indicating a market move to a downtrend.

Toronto Futures Exchange/Toronto Stock Exchange (TFE/TSE)
Twinned Canadian exchanges which list contracts on stock indices and equity options.

touch
The best buying and selling (bid and offer) prices available from market-makers on SEAQ and on SEAQ International in a particular security at the current time. On SEAQ, these appear in a yellow strip above the full quote displays of all registered market-makers in that stock.

trade balance
The difference between a nation's imports and exports of merchandise.

trade dispute
A situation arising where two traders disagree about a particular trade. This is normally arbitrated by an exchange official.

trade execution
The process by which orders are traded on the market floor via open outcry. (Except EFPs).

trade member
See **associate trade member**.

trade out
A brief period of time at the end of official trading hours in which unsatisfied orders can be settled at the closing price or within the closing range.

trade price
The price agreed between buyer and seller in the trading pit at which the transaction is executed. This is the price at which at any point in time the

last trade was made, whether it was a buyer taking the ask price or a seller taking the bid price.

trade share
A procedure or convention on certain markets whereby multiple acceptors of a counterparty offer, or bid, agree to share the market volume available in order to avoid dispute as to who might have been the first to accept the market quotation.

trading hours
The hours when a particular contract is open for trading.

trading limit[1]
The maximum futures position any individual is allowed to hold at any time under CFTC or exchange regulations. *See also* **position limit**.

trading limit[2]
Prices above or below which trading is not allowed during any one day.

trading strategies
See under long or short position name.

traditional options
A London Stock Exchange quasi-American-style option bargain that has a maximum life of seven accounts and is exercisable only on the declaration day (second Thursday) in each account. Puts, calls and double options are available from option dealers but there is no secondary trading market. They may be sold back to the original counterparty.

trading range
The range of prices that have been traded over a particular period of time.

transaction
A single deal, irrespective of the number of contracts traded.

transfer form
A form signed by the seller of a share or corporate bond authorizing the registrar to remove his or her name from the register and substitute that of the buyer.

transferable notice
A notice signifying the intention to make actual delivery. This is given by the seller of a futures contract.

transfer trades
Entries made upon the books of futures commission merchants for the purpose of (a) transferring existing trades from one account to another within the same office where no change in ownership is involved; (b) transferring existing trades from the books of one commission merchant to the books of another commission merchant, where no change in ownership is involved; (c) exchanging futures for cash commodities; or (d) exchanging futures positions, one of which was taken to fix the price of a commodity involved in a call sale. (US)

Treasury bill
A short-term government debt instrument with a maturity of one year or less. Bills are sold at a discount from par with the interest earned being the difference between the face value received at maturity and the price paid.

Treasury bond
See **US Treasury bond**.

Treasury note
See **US Treasury note**.

Treasury note contracts
Futures and options contracts on US Treasury notes. these work in exactly the same manner as for long-term interest rate contracts.

trend
The general direction in which prices are moving.

trend channel
An area on a price chart between a trendline and a return line.

trendline
A line drawn on a technical analysis chart either below a rising trend (*support line*) or above a falling trend (*resistance line*).

triangles
Chart patterns. See **ascending, descending** and **symmetrical triangles**.

trigger option
Also a limit option. See **barrier option**.

triple top (triple bottom)
A chart pattern that is a rare and powerful variant of a head and shoulders reversal pattern.

trough
A low point in market price history.

TRS
Trade Registration System. Introduced by LIFFE and now extended to LCE and IPE. It is a real-time dual-sided matching and account assignment system which allows traders actively to confirm trades.

TSE
See **Tokyo Stock Exchange** or **Toronto Stock Exchange**.

tunnel
See **cylinder**.

Twin Cities Board of Trade
A US exchange, based in Minneapolis, which lists a currency cross-rate future.

two by one ratio call (put) spread
A call or (put) ratio backspread.

two-day reversal
A key day reversal pattern where the reversal signals are given over two days.

U

Ucits
'Undertaking for Collective Investments in Transactable Securities', an EC terminology for certain investment funds.

unallocated bullion holding accounts
With unallocated holding accounts, specific bars are not set aside but the client enjoys a general entitlement to a number of ounces of gold or silver. The costs of maintaining such accounts are at the discretion of the listed institution. See allocated bullion holding accounts.

uncovered call option
A short call option position without a holding of the underlying asset.

uncovered position
Alternative term for **open interest**.

uncovered put option
A short put option position where the writer is not short the underlying asset.

underlying commodity
The commodity or futures contract on which an option is based.

underlying futures contract
The specific futures contract that is bought or sold by exercising an option.

under reference (foreign exchange and currency deposit markets)
A deal cannot be finalized without reference to the principal which placed the order.

unmatched trade
A trade alleged by one market party but for which no counterparty claim (albeit, possibly a mismatching claim) is declared.

under reference (sterling deposits)
When principals puts brokers 'under reference', or puts them 'under reference', having previously put them 'firm', brokers should refer to the principals before they passes their names. If brokers quote prices 'under

reference', they must have the opportunity to check with one of their principals before being expected to deal in a marketable amount. (*Bank of England Grey Book*).

unsettled contract
A contract in respect of which the obligations of the parties have not been discharged, whether by performance, set-off or otherwise. It remains an open contract.

up-and-in option
See **barrier option**.

Up-and-out Option
See **barrier option**.

USD
Standard foreign exchange code for United States dollar(s).

USDA
United States Department of Agriculture.

US Treasury bill
Often called a *T-bill*, it is a discount security with a maturity of less than one year.

US Treasury bond
Often called a *T-bond*, it is a government debt security that pays coupons and with a maturity of more than 10 years. Interest is paid semi-annually.

US Treasury note
Often called a *T-note*, it is a government debt security that pays coupons and with a maturity of one to 10 years. Interest is paid semi-annually.

V

value basis
The difference between the fair futures price and the actual futures price. It thus indicates whether the future trades cheap or dear to its fair value. The actual basis is the sum of carry basis and value basis.

Vancouver Stock Exchange (VSE)
A Canadian exchange which lists gold and equity options.

vanishing options
A down and out option. *See* under **barrier option**.

variable limit
According to US exchange's rules, an expanded allowable price range set during volatile markets. *See also* **price limit**.

variation margin
The margin that must be supplied by holders of open contracts that are showing a loss on the last day's price movement. The profits and losses resulting from marking to market daily are paid over from 'losers' margin accounts to 'winners' accounts on a daily basis. This ensures that 'losers' can bear their losses. It is the accumulation of daily variation margin in the margin account that provides the profits when a position is profitably closed. Except on the LME and TIFFE, variation margin profits may be withdrawn prior to a contract being closed.

Vasicek option pricing model
An interest rate option pricing model. It does not guarantee consistency with the initial term structure. It has mean reversion.

vega
A measure of the rate of change in theoretical option price due to changes in the volatility of the underlying asset price. It is generally quoted in points per percentage change in volatility. It is at its highest when an option is at the money and decreases as the market price moves away from the exercise price. Options closer to expiry have a higher vega than those with more time remaining. Positions with a positive vega are generally associated with positive gamma and positive theta.

verbal contract
The basis on which markets that trade by open outcry initially establish their legal, contractual rights and obligations within the contracts traded.

versus cash
See **exchange for physicals.**

vertical spread
Buying and selling puts or calls of the same expiration month but different strike prices.

video/audio surveillance
Video cameras and microphones which record all trading activity on the market floor and may by viewed as an aid to settling disputed trades.

visible supply
Usually refers to supplies of a commodity in licensed warehouses. Often includes afloat and all other supplies 'in sight' in producing areas.

voice line
A telephone line (either public network or a private/dedicated circuit) that carries voice communication as opposed to data or electronic signal.

voice log
Multi channel recording equipment used by exchanges and their members to record instructions and investment advice carried on voice lines.

volatility
A measurement of the variability rate (but not the direction) of the change in price over a given time period. It is often expressed as a percentage and computed as the annualized standard deviation of percentage change in daily price. This is usually calculated as the annualized standard deviation of the natural log of the ratio of two successive prices. The more volatile the futures price the greater the time value and hence the option premium. *See* **historical volatility, implied volatility, forecast volatility, future volatility.**

volatility surface
A three-dimensional surface created by plotting option implied volatility (vertical axis) against exercise prices (horizontal axis) over time (third axis).

'volatility trade'
Long puts and long future, or long calls and short future, so long as each position is delta neutral. Net position will look like a straddle.

volatility trading

Traders may take a view that the volatility implied by an option price is too low—hence the option too cheap—and they will buy the option, or that it is too high and hence they will sell the option. Traders buy and sell volatility by buying and selling options respectively and delta hedging the directional risk. The total exposure to volatility of a position is measured by the weighted average of vega. A positive vega position is used if a rise in volatility is anticipated and a negative vega if a fall is foreseen. The classic volatility trades involve straddles and strangles established to delta neutrality.

VSE
See **Vancouver Stock Exchange**.

volume

The number of contracts executed for a given period (usually a day) in any given instrument or market. Volume in the UK is normally an expression of net contracts traded, e.g. Trader *A* sells 1 contract, and Trader *B* buys 1 contract, this would represent a market volume of 1 contract although in practice 2 separate open contract positions may have been established. These figures are used by technical analysts as a further guide to interpreting price patterns. Exchanges will also publish monthly and annual volume data and these are used to indicate liquidity in that market.

V-top
See **spike top**.

W

warehouse (exchange-approved)
Any location having storage, with adequate security provided, which has been inspected and approved by an exchange for registration as an approved warehouse. Warehouses may be in several categories, e.g., free-port or 'outside customs territory'; bonded or 'within customs territory' yet able to hold goods on which import duty or import VAT have not yet been levied; transit, which is comparable to bonded; or inland, where duty, etc. has been paid on goods stored.

warehouse receipt[1]
Document guaranteeing the existence and availability of a given quantity and quality of a commodity in storage; commonly used as the instrument of transfer of ownership in both cash and futures transactions.

warehouse receipt[2]
A receipt for a commodity given by a licensed or authorized warehouse and issued as a tender on futures contracts.

warrant (warehouse)
Document of title issued by warehouse conferring title to a set parcel of goods to the person named on the face of the document. The warrant may at any time be endorsed to another nominee or to 'bearer', making it a readily negotiable document from the standpoint of its use as collateral for bank finance, etc. Warrants are the accepted documents for delivery on certain futures markets.

warrant
A stock market security with a market price of its own that can be converted into a specific share at a predetermined price and date. The value of the warrant is thus determined by the premium (if any) of the share price over the conversion price of the warrant. There are also warrants available on gold and oil, where they are convertible into these commodities.

wash sale
A fictitious transaction usually made so it will appear that there are, or have been, trades, but without a position in the market actually being taken. Such sales are prohibited by the US Commodity Exchange Act.

WCE
See **Winnipeg Commodity Exchange**.

"what's bid?"
A pit trader's challenge to the market to establish the bids and contract volume in a contract.

"what's offered?"
The same as "what's bid" except that it relates to offers as opposed to bids.

"what's there?"
A pit traders challenge to establish both current bids and offers.

weak hands
When used in connection with delivery of commodities on futures contracts, the term usually means that the party probably does not intend to retain ownership of the commodity; when used in connection with futures positions, the term usually means positions held by small speculators.

wedge
A chart-reversal pattern that is a trendline and record line converging. This usually results in a trendline break. There are both falling and rising wedges and they can be continuation patterns too.

wet barrels
Oil trading term signifying delivery of a product rather than the transfer of a tanker receipt.

wet market
Market in physical oil, as distinct from paper market.

Whaley option pricing model
Option pricing model that models American option values using quadratic equations.

when issued (WI)
Trades before issuance, in which settlement occurs when and if the Treasury or agency issues the certificate or bond. These occur in the period between the announcement of a security's auction and its issuance.

Winnipeg Commodity Exchange
A Canadian exchange which lists contracts on barley, canola, flax, oats, rye and feed.

Winter wheat
Wheat that is planted in the autumn, lies dormant during the winter, and is harvested in June and July of the next year.

wire house
See **futures commission merchant (FCM)**.

withholding tax
The income tax deducted from the coupon of a bond when payment is made net. Also the tax deducted by one country on payments of coupons or dividends paid overseas. In this latter case this may be subject to a bilateral tax treaty or double tax relief.

writer
See **options seller**.

WTI
West Texas Intermediate (oil).

Y

yellow jacket
On LIFFE, an alternative name for a runner or RFC, so called because of the colour of jacket that such personnel are required to wear on the market floor.

yield
A measure of the annual return on an investment.

yield curve
A chart in which the yield level is plotted on the vertical axis and the term to maturity of debt instruments of similar creditworthiness (normally government bonds) is plotted on the horizontal axis. The yield curve is positive when long-term rates are higher than short-term rates. However, when short-term rates are higher than yields on long-term investments, the yield curve is negative or inverted.

yield-to-maturity
The return obtained on holding a bond to maturity. The yield-to-maturity assumes that any coupon payments received before redemption can be reinvested at this yield. This implies a flat yield curve and is hence not a realistic assumption.

yours (foreign exchange and currency deposit markets)
Opposite to **mine**.

Z

zero-cost options
Any strategy where the premium income on one option offsets premium expenditure on a bought option, both operations taking place simultaneously. *See* **synthetic long and short futures, collars, participating cap, participating forward**.

zero-coupon bond
A bond that has no coupon payments, just a single maturity payment. It will be sold at a discount to face value and will be more volatile than a coupon carrying bond of the same maturity or yield.

zeta
Same as **vega**.

APPENDICES

Appendices

Appendix 1 193
Option premium value components (call option)

Appendix 2 194
Option strategy profit and loss diagrams

Appendix 3 198
Option pricing model output

Appendix 4 200
Profile of a call option vs. underlying price

Appendix 5 203
Position characteristics

Appendix 6 204
Characteristics of volatility spreads

Appendix 7 205
Evaluating a position

Appendix 1

Option premium value components (call option)

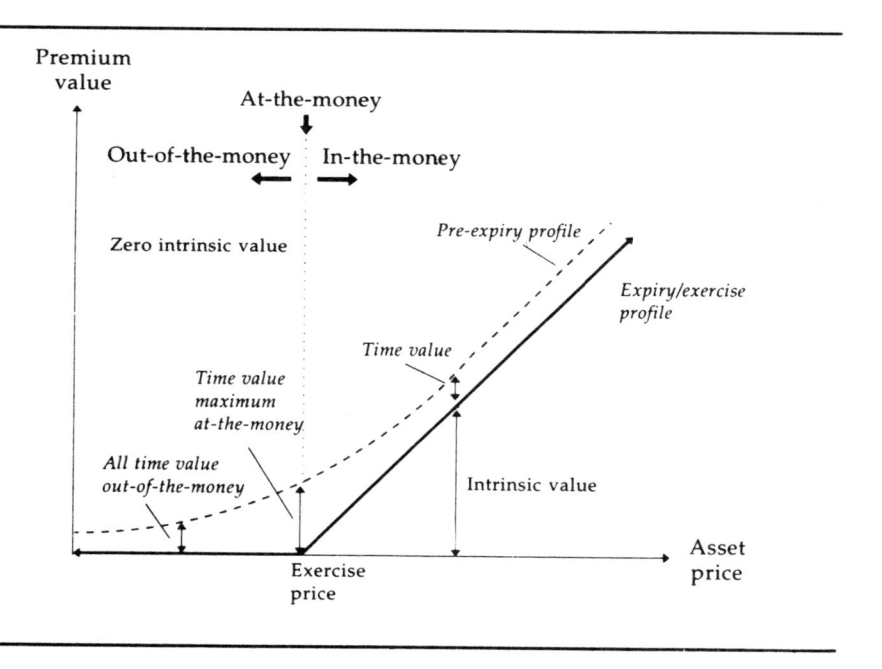

Appendix 2

Option strategy profit and loss diagrams

at expiry —— *prior to expiry* - - - -

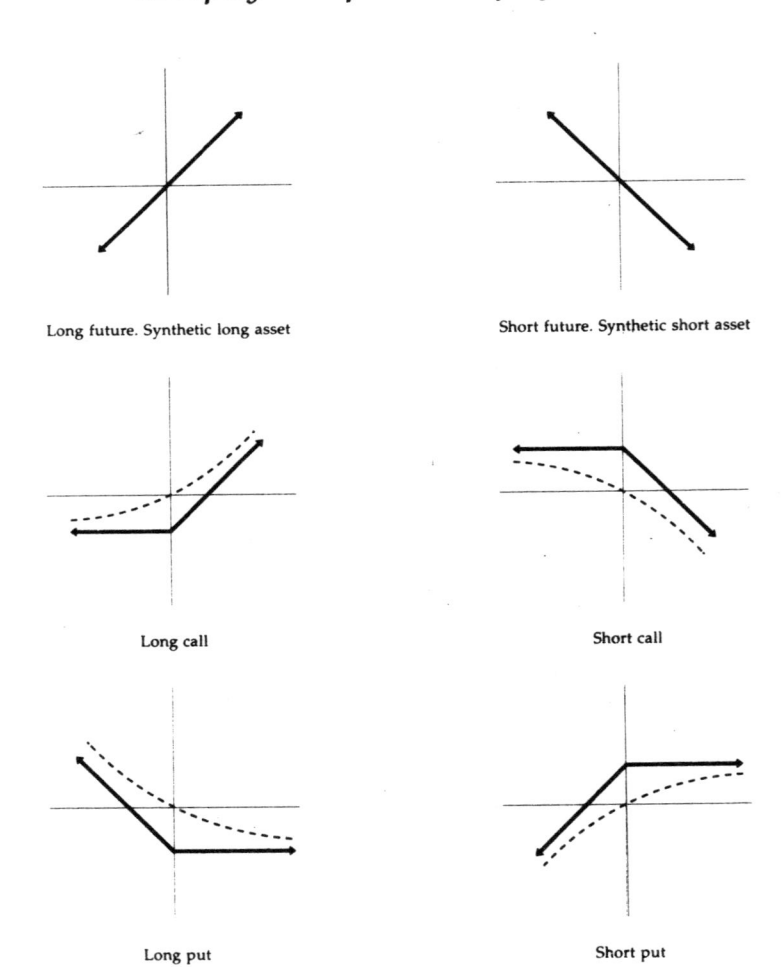

Long future. Synthetic long asset

Short future. Synthetic short asset

Long call

Short call

Long put

Short put

Option strategy profit and loss diagrams (cont.)

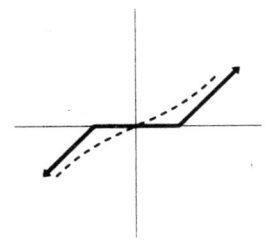

Synthetic long future (split strike) & bull cylinder

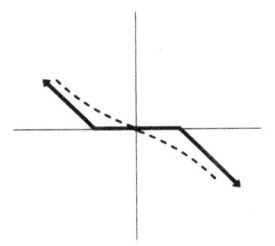

Synthetic short future (split strike), or combo or bear cylinder

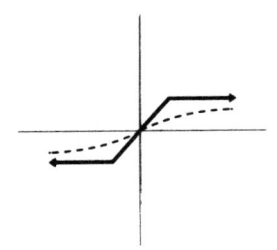

Bull spread

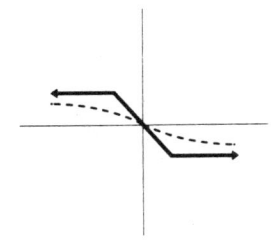

Bear spread

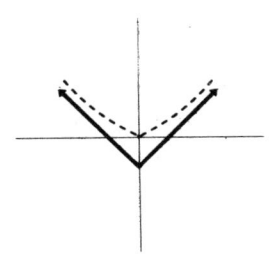

Long straddle

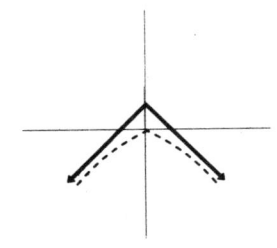

Short straddle

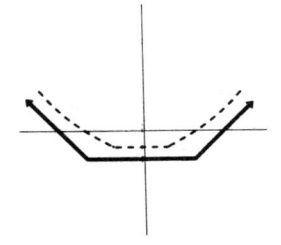

Long strangle, combination or guts

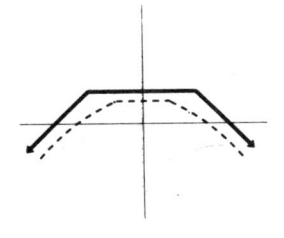

Short strangle, combination or guts

Option strategy profit and loss diagrams (cont.)

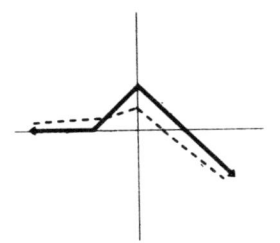

Call ratio spread

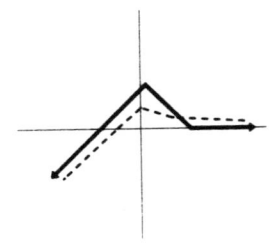

Put ratio spread

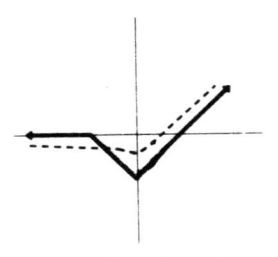

Call ratio backspread or two by one ratio call spread

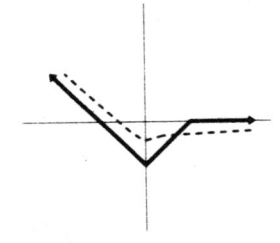

Put ratio backspread or two by one ratio put spread

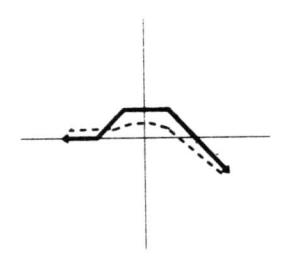

Call table top or ladder

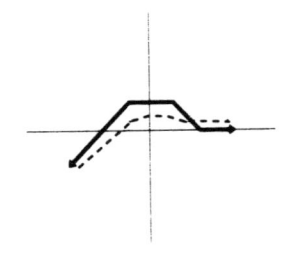

Put table top or ladder

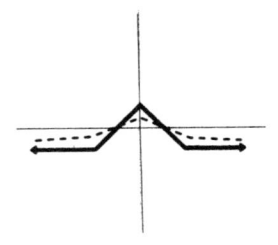

Long butterfly

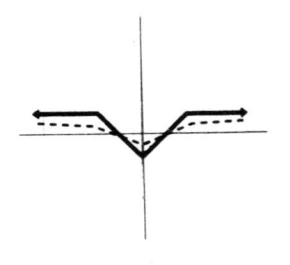

Short butterfly

Option strategy profit and loss diagrams (cont.)

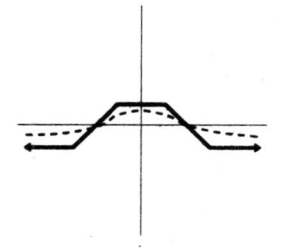

Long condor

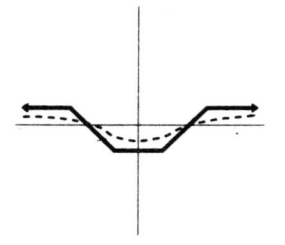

Short condor

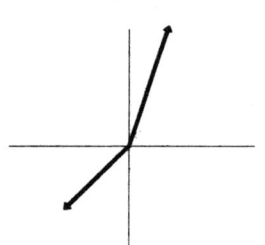

Long Texas 'hedge'

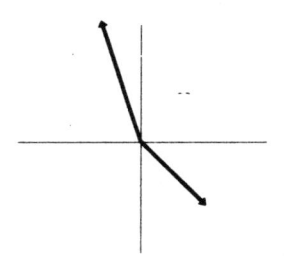

Short Texas 'hedge'

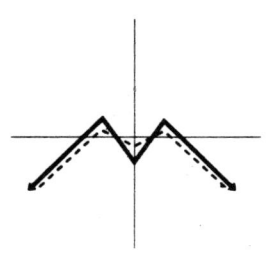

'Mae West'

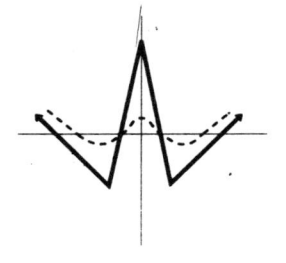

Mexican hat

Appendix 3

Option pricing model output

All option pricing models, whether they be based on Black-Scholes or binomial approaches, have the same inputs. These are:

- Current underlying asset price
- Exercise or strike price
- Time to expiry
- Short term interest rates
- Expected volatility

All these inputs are known with certainty except the expected volatility which will be a forecast estimate. If it is changed all output results of the model will change. The model is capable of producing figures for the following:

Premium = Price of an option

$$delta\ (\delta) = \frac{change\ in\ option\ premuim}{change\ in\ underlying}$$

Delta values range from 0 - 1 (or 0 - 100), and are about 0.5 (or 50) at the money. As time passes, or volatility assumptions change, deltas move away from 0.5 (or 50).

$$delta\ hedge\ ratio = \frac{value\ of\ asset\ to\ be\ hedged}{contract\ value of\ asset} \times \frac{1}{\delta}$$

This hedge ratio will need adjusting as delta changes. Delta will change as the underlying moves, volatility estimates change, or time passes. If the asset to be hedged is an option then the top line should be re-written as *value of asset to be hedged × delta of asset*.

is an option then the top line should be re-written as *value of asset to be hedged × delta of asset*.

$$^1gamma\ (\gamma) = \frac{change\ in\ option\ delta}{change\ in\ underlying}$$

Gamma (curvature) is always greatest at the money. As time to expiry gets shorter, or the volatility assumption is decreased, the gamma can increase dramatically.

$$vega\ (v) = \frac{point\ change\ in\ theoretical\ option\ value}{change\ in\ underlying\ volatility}$$

Vega decreases as time to expiry grows shorter. Longer maturity options will always be more sensitive to changes in volatility than short maturity options. Options have their greatest vega at the money but, out of the money options have the greatest vega as a per cent of their theoretical value.

$$theta\ (\theta) = points\ lost\ in\ theoretical\ option\ value\ per\ day$$

Theta increases as expiry approaches, and the premium of short maturity options decays faster than long maturity options. Theta is greatest at the money.

$$rho\ (\rho) = sensitivity\ of\ an\ option's\ theoretical\ value\ to\ changes\ in\ interest\ rates$$

Note that all of the above are derived from option pricing models, dependent upon the volatility assumption input, and will be good only for small changes in the value of the underlying asset.

---

[1] *Gamma and theta go hand in hand. A large positive gamma will also have a large positive theta (assuming a long position is regarded as having positive theta).*

Appendix 4

Profile of a call option vs. underlying price

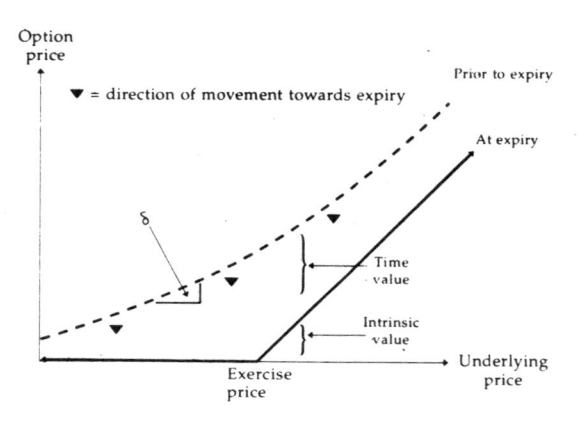

Call premium value against underlying price

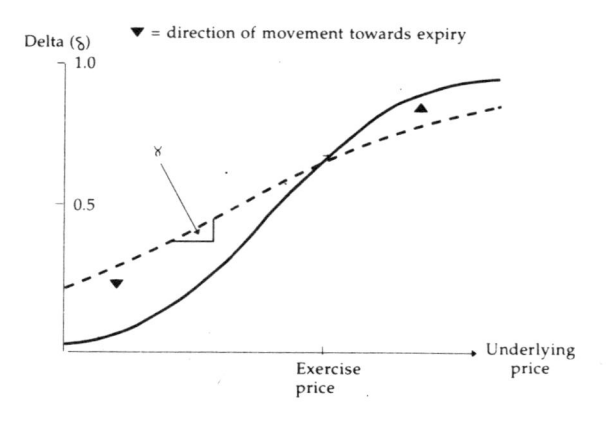

Call delta against underlying price

Appendices 201

Profile of a call option vs. underlying price (cont.)

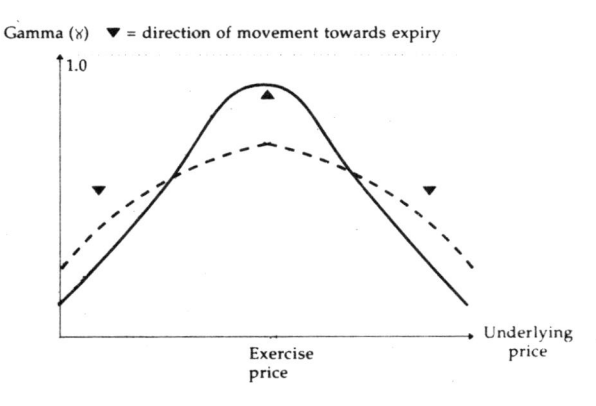

Gamma (ɤ) ▼ = direction of movement towards expiry

1.0

Exercise price

Underlying price

Call gamma against underlying price

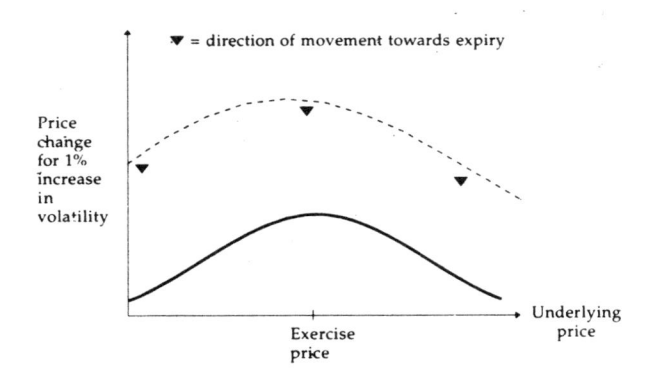

▼ = direction of movement towards expiry

Price change for 1% increase in volatility

Exercise price

Underlying price

Premium change for a 1% change in call volatility against underlying price

Profile of a call option vs. underlying price (cont.)

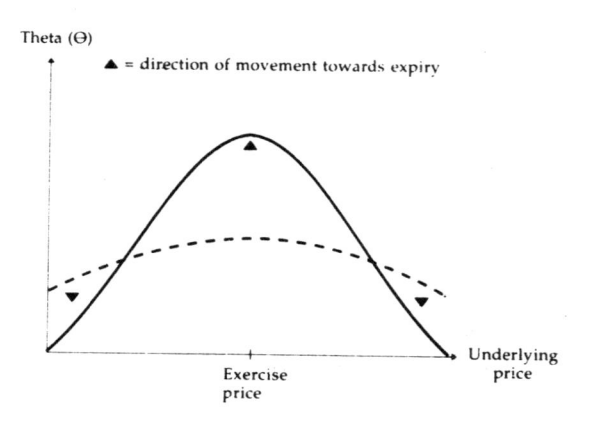

Change in call option value as time passes against underlying price

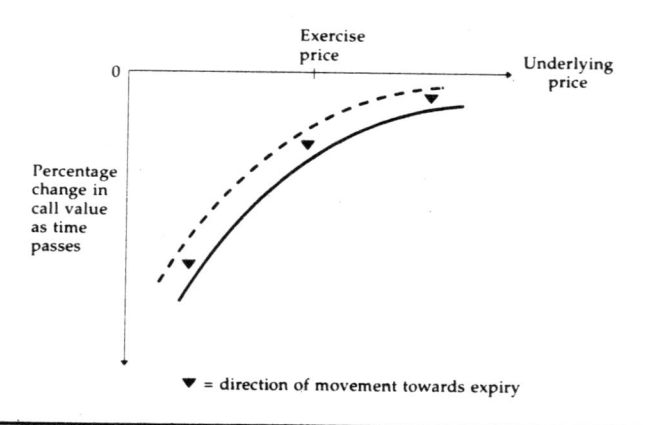

Percentage change in call option value as time passes against underlying price

Appendix 5

Position characteristics

No matter how complex a position is, with many options at different exercise prices and expiry dates, it can be summarized overall in terms of its delta, gamma, vega and theta. This allows its exposure to underlying price movement, to changes in volatility and to the passage of time to be readily assessed.

Position	Delta (hedge ratio)	Gamma (curvature)	Vega (volatility)	Theta* (time decay)	Rho (interest effect)
Long asset	Positive	0	0	0	0
Short asset	Negative	0	0	0	0
Long call	Positive	Positive	Positive	Positive	Positive
Short call	Negative	Negative	Negative	Negative	Negative
Long put	Negative	Positive	Positive	Positive	Negative
Short put	Positive	Negative	Negative	Negative	Positive

* *Positive time decay works against long position holder*

If position delta is:
Positive
Negative

Desired movement in underlying:
Rise in price
Fall in price

If position gamma is:
Positive
Negative

Desired movement in underlying:
Make large move
Be static

If position vega is:
Positive
Negative

Desired movement in volatility:
Rise
Fall

If position theta* is:
Positive
Negative

Passage of time will:
Harm position
Help position

* *Long option position considered to have positive theta*

Appendix 6

Characteristics of volatility spreads

Spread type	Delta position	Gamma position	Theta position	Vega position
Call backspread	0	+	+	+
Put backspread	0	+	+	+
Long straddle	0	+	+	+
Long strangle	0	+	+	+
Short butterfly	0	+	+	+
Short condor	0	+	+	+
Call ratio spread	0	-	-	-
Put ratio spread	0	-	-	-
Short straddle	0	-	-	-
Short strangle	0	-	-	-
Long butterfly	0	-	-	-
Long condor	0	-	-	-
Long time spread	0	-	-	+
Short time spread	0	+	+	-

Appendices 205

Appendix 7

Evaluating a position

Consider the following simplified page display:

- Asset price = 100.00; time to expiration = 60 days; volatility = 30%; interest = 8.00%

CALLS

Exercise price	Price	Theoretical value	Delta	Gamma	Theta	Vega
90	11.26	11.08	81	2.1	.024	.10
95	8.05	7.54	68	2.9	.034	.14
100	4.95	4.79	52	3.2	.039	.16
105	2.79	2.83	36	3.1	.037	.15
110	1.38	1.56	23	2.5	.030	.12

PUTS

Exercise price	Price	Theoretical value	Delta	Gamma	Theta	Vega
90	1:25	1.22	-18	2.1	.026	.10
95	3.02	2.61	-31	2.9	.035	.14
100	4.83	4.79	-47	3.2	.039	.16
105	7.63	7.76	-63	3.1	.036	.15
110	11.15	11.43	-76	2.5	.029	.12

An options trader sets up a long butterfly, comprised of being long a 95 put, short a 100 call and 100 put and long a 105 call. What exactly is the trader's position and where will it provide a profit/loss and break-even?

It is a rule that the expiry profile will be composed of straight lines and that the profile will bend at the exercise prices. Consider the situation for the trader for each option at each price for the underlying asset at expiry (see overleaf).

Cont.

Cont.

P=premium Expiry level of asset	Long 95 put	Short 100 call	Short 100 put	Long 100 call	Total
90					
Exercised	Yes	No	Yes	No	
Profit/loss	1.98 (5.00-3.02)	4.95 (P)	-5.17 (4.83-10.00)	-2.79 (P)	-1.03
95					
Exercised	No	No	Yes	No	
Profit/loss	-3.02 (P)	4.95 (P)	-0.17 (4.83-5.00)	-2.79 (P)	-1.03
100					
Exercised	No	No	No	No	
Profit/loss	-3.02 (P)	4.95 (P)	4.83 (P)	-2.79 (P)	3.97
105					
Exercised	No	Yes	No	No	
Profit/loss	-3.02 (P)	-0.05 (4.95-5.00)	4.83 (P)	-2.79 (P)	-1.03
110					
Exercised	No	Yes	No	Yes	
Profit/loss	-3.02 (P)	-5.05 (4.95-10.00)	4.83 (P)	2.21 (5.00-2.79)	-1.03

This can thus be sketched as:

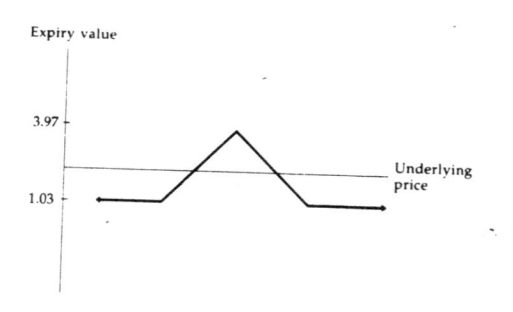

It is known as a 'long butterfly'. Maximum loss at 95 or below or 105 and above, of 1.03. Maximum profit is 3.97 at underlying price of 100 *at expiry*. Changes in volatility, delta, time to expiry etc., may alter the position value prior to expiry.

To establish effects on position of such changes first calculate position cost, delta, gamma, vega, theta.

	Cost	Theoretical value	Delta	Gamma	Theta	Vega
Long 95 put	-3.02	-2.61	-31	+2.9	+0.035	+0.14
Short 100 call	+4.95	+4.79	-52	-3.2	-0.039	-0.16
Short 100 put	+4.83	+4.79	+47	-3.2	-0.039	-0.16
Long 105 call	-2.79	-2.83	+36	+3.1	+0.037	+0.15
Position total:	+3.97	+4.14	0	-0.4	-0.006	-0.03

Theoretical edge

The first point to note here is that the cost of the position in the market is 3.97, the theoretical value is 4.14. Therefore the position is cheap, with a theoretical edge of 0.17

From these figures the new position value can be established under a variety of conditions.

Delta and underlying price change

If the underlying asset price moves, by a small amount only, then assuming no change in the time to expiry or in volatility, the value of the position will remain at 3.97.

Had a different position been established, not delta neutral, but had a delta of, say, 75, then since the delta is given by:

$$\delta = \frac{\text{change in option value}}{\text{change in asset price}}$$

then, if the underlying asset rose to, say, 102, the change in the position value is given by:

change in position value = δ (*change in asset price*)

and, in this example,

$$\text{change in position value} = \frac{75}{100}(102-100)$$

$$= 1.5$$

and hence the new position value is 3.97 + 1.5 = 5.47. Positive delta gives a positive gain in position value as the underlying rises. If the delta value had been -75 then the new position would be worth 2.47.

Gamma and delta

Similarly, since gamma is the rate of change of delta in relation to the underlying, if the underlying rises in price by 2, then assuming no change in volatility etc. the new delta value will be given by:

$$\text{new delta} = -0.4 \, (1.02 - 100) - \text{original delta}$$

$$= -0.8$$

Theta and the passage of time

Theta can be used to calculate the position value change with the passage of time. If three trading days pass and no change occurs in the underlying price or the volatility then the position value is given by:

$$3.97 + (-3 \times (-0.006)) = 3.988$$

The passage of time helps the position.

Vega and volatility changes

Vega measures the responsiveness of the position to changes in the volatility of the underlying. Volatility is 30%. If it rises to 34% then the position value will change by:

$$4\% \times (-0.03) = -0.12$$

and the new position value is 3.85.

To establish a delta neutral position

If a trader took a view that volatility was going to decline by 5% he might establish a short straddle to delta neutrality using short calls and puts with strike or exercise prices of 100. If he sells X calls and Y puts then, using the previous chart

$$\text{Position } \delta = 0 \;\; = \;\; -X\,(52) - Y\,(-47)$$

$$\delta = 0 \;\; = \;\; 47Y - 52X$$

and so, 47 calls and 52 puts would provide a delta neutral position, or any larger multiple thereof (i.e. short 94 calls and 104 puts).

The premium income on this position would be:

47 × 4.95
52 × 4.83
―――――
483.31

The theoretical value is:

47 × 4.79
52 × 4.79
―――――
474.21

So the theoretical edge is +9.1

The position vega is:

47 × −0.16
52 × −0.16
―――――
−15.84

So if volatility does fall by 5% then the position value will be changed by:

(5) × (−15.84) = −79.2

Allowing the position to be closed out at 404.11 with a profit of 79.2.

Acknowledgements

I would like to acknowledge the assistance of the following persons in the preparation of this material: Patrick Thompson, *Derivative Solutions*; Martin Cooper, *Chase Manhattan*; Keith Redhead, *Coventry University*; Graham Wright, *GWAssociates*; Ken Heymer, *Independent Consultant*; Gordon Gemmill, *City University Business School*; Petros Geroulanos, *Guildhall Ltd.*; Nick Battley.

I would like to acknowledge especially the use made of *The Chase Guide to Risk Management Products* published for Chase Manhattan Bank by Risk Magazine Ltd. in respect of entries for a number of the more sophisticated option products now available off-exchange.

Needless to say, I must claim responsibility for all remaining errors.

Alan Webber

THE PROFESSIONAL INVESTOR

The world's best books for institutional investors, fund managers, equity analysts & traders

How to Build a Stock Market Fortune the Way World's Most Successful Professionals do

Now, you can benefit from the investment strategies and trading tactics used by the top international fund managers and investment professionals who handle and amass fortunes in the global stock markets.

Presented on the following pages are state-of-the-art professional investment books with brief write-ups and expert reviews to help you select the books you may need.

Not just that. In collaboration with leading international publishers, Vision Books is able to offer you special Indian reprints of many of these books at very attractive prices which are often 75% less than their international prices.

Even where only imported editions are available, these too often come to you at special prices.

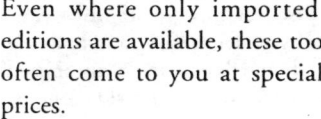

Exclusive Customer Privilege Offer
➤ 15% off on purchases above Rs. 1,000;
➤ 10% off on purchases between Rs. 395 - Rs. 1,000!

So rush your order using the enclosed *Customer Privilege Voucher* enclosed in the book or by letter, with your bank draft in favour of Vision Books Pvt. Ltd. and we will immediately send you the world's best investment books of your choice. (*See* page 8 for details of the exclusive customer privilege offer).

DERIVATIVES TRADING

How to Make Money Trading Derivatives
An Insider's Giide
Ashwani Gujral

BESTSELLER — 2nd EDITION — 5,000+ COPIES SOLD

This is a pioneering book on trading derivatives in the Indian market. The book focuses on:

- Technical tools for derivatives traders and how to use them
- Profitable day trading strategies and methods
- Cash and futures arbitrage for making profits from idle cash
- Profitable futures trading strategies
- Options trading strategies that work in the Indian market
- Factors affecting options premium
- Figuring out when options are cheap — and when they are expensive
- High returns from covered call writing strategies
- Trading during special events, such as elections, company results.
- Trading discipline and money management.

Plus: 2 New Chapters
- Selection of Stocks and Futures
- My Trading Diary — The Bubble and the Crash (February-June 2006).

"Gujral has cemented himslef as a pioneer in the field."
— James Holter, Editor, Futures Magazine, USA

Rs. 395/- No. 682-3

FUTURES & OPTIONS

Profit in the Futures Markets!
Insights and Strategies for Futures and Futures Options Trading: Jake Bernstein

Filled with practical tools and techniques for understanding and prospering in the world of futures trading, *Profit in the Futures Markets!* shows how to use such information to your best advantage. In addition, you will discover how to improve your trading strategies by understanding and building upon your own style and developing a customized plan for success based on your individual needs and abilities.

Investors interested in expanding into the potentially lucrative world of futures need look no further than this easy-to-read, insight-filled guide.

"Jake Bernstein is one of the best at putting together the emotions and mechanics of trading"
Futures Magazine, USA

"One of the best books I've ever seen on the futures markets" Rick Bensignor Chief Technical Strategist, Morgan Stanley

"This exceptional book fast forwards the learning curve..." Adrienne Laris Toghraie, Trader's Success Coach

Rs. 395/- No.520-8

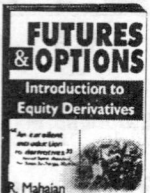

Futures and Options
Introduction to Equity Derivatives
R. Mahajan
BEST SELLER

Derivatives include futures and options and are an indispensable part and parcel of developed financial markets. How deriva-tives work and how you can benefit from them to protect your stock market investment is the thrust of this book.

The book covers both futures and options and risk-proofing tools available to the Indian investor. The author explains both the underlying concepts and procedures in a straightforward manner.

Assuming no prior knowledge, both beginners and market operators will find this an easy-to-understand book to get started in futures and options.

"The book draws the reader into this esorteric subject with lucid writing style and simple examples, and tries to explain the *raison d'être* of futures and options" *Business India*

"An excellent introduction to derivatives for all market participants and investors" Anand Rathi, President, The Stock Exchange, Mumbai.

Rs. 280/- No. 691-3

Dictionary of Futures & Options
Over 1,500 Terms Defined and Explained
Alan Webber

The *Dictionary of Futures & Options* is a comprehensive reference source of essential information for any investor involved in futures and options. Both the complete beginner and the seasoned professional will find this book invaluable. It contains all the basic terminology used throughout the international derivatives arena, as well as substantial descriptions of options strategies, the "Greek" letters, position exposure to certain measures, and more.

In addition, the appendices include graphics which will enable interested readers to absorb the intricacies of various derivative trading scenarios in a quick, but thorough, manner.

"Reference book on futures & options" *The Hindu*

Rs. 395/- No. 331-0

New Insights on Writing Covered Call Options
The Powerful Technique that Enhances Return and Lowers Risk in Stock Investing
Richard Lehman and Lawrence G. McMillan
BEST SELLER

Writing covered call options is an investment strategy that bridges the gap between equity and fixed-income investments.

It offers much of the upside potential of equities — but with less volatility. Thus, you can achieve long-term returns commensurate with stock market returns but with lower volatility and less downside risk.

This book shows how to use this powerful and accessible investment technique — giving you the edge to enhance your returns and lower your risk.

"This book makes a great case for basic reading and writting --- reading stock charts and writing covered calls"
John Murphy

Rs. 395/- No. 555-0

TECHNICAL ANALYSIS

Timing the Market
BEST SELLER
How to Profit in Bull & Bear Markets with Technical Analysis
Curtis M. Arnold
"For the savvy investor" *Business Today*
"The Bible of technical analysis!" *MBH Commodity Advisors, USA*
Rs. 280/- No. 662-X

Using Technical Analysis: The Basics
Cliford Pistolese
"Enables investors to take profitable decisions" *Business India*
Rs. 190/- No. 391-4

International Encyclopedia of Technical Analysis
Joel G. Seigel, Jae K. Shim, Anique Qureshi, Jeffrey Brauchier
A-to-Z of Technical Analysis for trading stocks, derivatives and Commodities
Rs. 495/- No. 648-4

The Psychology of Technical Analysis
Tony Plummer
"One of the most exciting and innovative books on technical analysis" *Market Technician, U.K.*
Rs. 395/- No. 492-9

Elliott Wave Explained
How to use the Elliott Wave System to Forecast Future Share Price Movements: Robert C. Beckman
A superb introduction to one of the best-performing forecasting methods ever devised. With real-life examples.
"Robert Beckman's forecasts of major market movements ... have shifted huge sums of money as institutions have been jerked into action." *Investor's Review, USA*
Rs. 395/- No. 532-1

Martin Pring on Market Momentum
BEST SELLER
Martin J. Pring
The A-to-Z of market momentum by one of the world's foremost technical analysts.
"Definitive guide to momentum" *Trader's Press, USA*
"A Bible on momentum" *The Economic Times*
Rs. 395/- No. 570-4

Technical Analysis for Futures Traders
A Comprehensive Guide to Analytical Methods, Trading Systems and Technical Indicators
Darrel R. Jobman
Technical Analysis for Futures Traders is a definitive book on the application of technical analysis for trading.
Rs. 495/- No.577-1

Candlestick Charting Explained
BEST SELLER
Timeless Techniques for Trading Stocks and Futures
Gregory L. Morris
"Arguably the best book on candles, tying them together, with technical analysis ..." *Technical Trends, USA*
Rs. 395/- No. 240-3

GREAT VALUE EDITION 80% LOWER THAN INTERNATIONAL PRICE

Technical Analysis of Stock Trends
BEST SELLER
Robert Edwards & John Magee
"This book is a classic — the standard of excellence against which everything in technical analysis is measured... learn from this wonderful book" *Prudential Securities, USA*
Rs. 595/- No. 663-8

Technical Analysis from A-to-Z
BEST SELLER
Steven B. Achelis
"All aspects of technical analysis in one easily digestible book ... belongs on every technician's bookshelf" *Steven Nison*
"Can be used as a dictionary for technical analysis" *Business Investor's Daily, USA*
Rs. 395/- No. 312-4

The Technical Analysis Course
BEST SELLER
A Winning Program for Investors & Traders
Thomas A. Meyers
This book highlights when, where, and how you can employ the variety of technical analysis tools available.
"Mastery to this arcane but widely followed art" *The Wall Street Journal, USA*
Rs. 325/- No. 489-9

Technical Analysis of Stocks, Options & Futures
Advanced Trading Systems and Techniques **BEST SELLER**
William F. Eng
This book provides detailed and practical information on fifteen of the most widely used trading systems.
"Encyclopedic in scope ... should be in every trader's library" *Leslie Rosenthal, Former Chairman, Chicago Board of Trade.*
Rs. 495/- No. 531-3

MUTUAL FUNDS

Indian Mutual Funds Handbook
A Guide for Industry Professionals and Intelligent Investors

Sundar Sankaran

This comprehensive handbook by an expert lays out the working of Indian mutual funds, their operational and regulatory mechanisms, the advantages and limitations of investing in them along with suitable approaches to personal financial planning. The author's experience of handling hundreds of training programmes ensures an engaging and easy to understand approach to mastering the subject.

Highlights: Benefits of investing in mutual funds; how they compare with bank and company fixed deposits and other investment avenues ■ The different types of equity, debt, balanced and liquid scheme available for investment — and the rewards and risks each one entails ■ NAV — what it reveals, its calculation and finer nuances ■ The costs of investing in mutual funds — loads, expenses and management fee.

"I recommend this book to everyone who wants to make informed investment decisions"
— Shekhar Sathe, Kotak Mahindra

"The best book for understanding (Indian) mutual funds"
— M. Subramanian CEO India, Barclays Bank, plc.

"If you think you know everything about mutual funds, read the book to find out how much you don't know!"
— Prof. G. Sethu, Dean, UTI Institute of Capital Markets

Rs. 190/- No. 536-4

The New Commonsense Guide to Mutual Funds: Mary Rowland

This book shows you how you can best use mutual funds to meet your financial goals.

This is a top-selling book, by one of America's pre-eminent financial journalists. It cuts through the hype and confusion surrounding mutual funds and tells you exactly what you need to know.

"Remarkable! A splendid combination of wisdom and simplicity" — John C. Bogle

"Nuts and bolts of fund investing, plus an excellent section on measuring an investor's tolerance for risk"
— The Wall Street Journal, USA

Rs. 280 No. 479-1

The Winning Portfolio
How to Choose the Best Mutual Funds: Paul B. Farrell

Farrell's strategy is easy-to-follow and will help you diversify your portfolio while shielding your investment in mutual funds from market downturns.

'An easy-to-follow roadmap for maximizing your mutual funds profits ... both rational and intuitive" — Brian Murray

"Eminently practical advice for selecting mutual funds"
— John C. Bogle

Rs. 190/- No. 481-3

POINT AND FIGURE CHARTING

The Complete Guide to Point and Figure Charting
A Manual of Charting and Trading Techniques

Heinrich Weber and Kermit Zieg

"Point-and-figure is the best of all technical analysis methods," assert the expert authors and demonstrate in this book how this method produces consistent and reliable trading profits.

"A natural 'primer' for new users, (with) plenty for the more experienced." — Dave Baker, PFscan Charting Software

""A masterpiece of clarity ... puts most treatments of technical analysis to shade" — Alexander Davidson

Rs. 595/- No. 670-0

ASSET ALLOCATION

Asset Allocation and Portfolio Optimization
Warren E. Bitters

A study of the late 1980s suggested that asset allocation policy alone explained as much as 93.6% of investment return. It implied that market timing and security selection are far less influential factors in determining total return. The startling conclusion led to tremendous focus on the importance of asset allocation in the investment management process. This book provides a comprehensive survey of the increasingly sophisticated methods which have since been developed and applied in this area.

Rs. 395/- No. 571-2

INVESTMENT BASICS

Investing for Beginners
Kathy Kristof

This book is simple. It's straightforward. It skilfully guides you step-by-step to investment success. Highlights: ■ Investment Risks and Rewards ■ Your Starting Point ■ How to pick stocks ■ Investing in Bonds ■ Mutual Funds Primer.

"Smart, sensible advice ... a road map to financial success without gimmicks or secret formulas."
Los Angeles Times, USA

Order No. 482-1
Price: Rs. 190/-

How to Manage Your Investment Risks & Returns
An Essential Self-teaching Guide for Every Investor
David L. Scott

The secret of successful investing lies rather in understanding and controlling the risk involved in any investment. Step-by-step this book shows you how to control your investment risks.

"An object lesson." *The Economic Times*

Order No. 394-9
Price: Rs. 145/-

INVESTMENT OPTIONS

Profitable investment in shares : *A Beginner's Guide*
S. S. Grewal & Navjot Grewal

This hugely popular book tells you the basic principles and guidelines of profitable investment in shares. It also highlights the basic rules to follow in order to ensure reasonable safety of your capital. And it does all this in simple, clear language without resorting to jargon or technicalities. So, if are you one of those who wants to invest in shares but doesn't know quite how to go about it, then you can't do much better than starting with this book.

"Positively rewarding." *Financial Express*

Order No. 573-9
Price: Rs. 145

The Basics of Investing
Gerald Krefetz

The rapidly growing number of investment avenues often lead to confusion. In this book, an investment expert offers you the must-know principles, expert guidance and sensible solutions to invest your money profitably.

Order No. 446-5
Price: Rs. 190

The Basics of Stocks
Gerald Krefetz

You probably need to invest in shares to achieve long-term capital appreciation. What you also need to do is to do it right. In simple, easy-to-follow steps, a Wall Street expert offers you solutions for making the most out of investing in shares.

Order No. 448-1
Price: Rs. 190

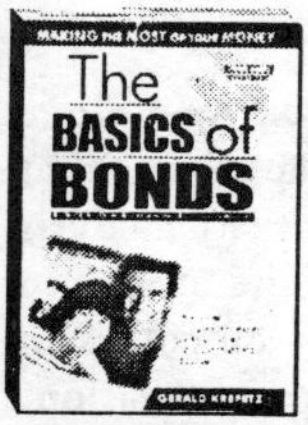

The Basics of Bonds
Profitable Fixed-Income Investing
Gerald Krefetz

The lure: bonds and other fixed income investment avenues offer relatively greater safety of capital with predict-able returns. This book by a U.S. investment expert will assist you in making intelligent decisions about your fixed-income investing.

Order No. 447-3
Price: Rs. 190

The Basics of Speculating
How to Speculate Most Profitably with Your Hard-Earned Money
Gerald Krefetz

This book tackles in detail the most popular financial instruments used for speculation: stocks, bonds, options, futures, commodities, precious metals and foreign exchange, etc.,

Order No. 449-X
Price: Rs. 190

INVESTMENT

The Financial Analyst's Handbook: What Practitioners Need to Know: Mark Kritzman

Mark Kritzman shows financial analysts and serious investors how to employ both sophisticated tools as well as common sense when evaluating past results and projecting future performance. Objective, practical and essential, the book covers the key concepts, methodology, and strategies inherent to thorough and rigorous investment analysis.

"Covers the key tools of modern investment practice ... valuable volume"
William F. Sharpe, Nobel Prize Winner

"Kritzman explains the tools in the financial analyst's toolbox with astounding clarity" Gary L. Gastineau

Rs. 395/- No. 563-1

Advanced Approaches to Stock Selection

Ross Paul Bruner, editor

This book explores contemporary investment concepts and tools for improving the stock selection process. The expert contributors examine various investment strategies organized around growth, value, size and sector rotation from a number of different perspectives. Price-momentum strategies, such as covariance and factor analysis, are also explored.

Rs. 395/- No. 572-0

Stock Market Logic

Norman G. Fosback

Some investors, utilizing more sophisticated approaches than the public at large, can earn above-average returns, year in and year out." This book will show you how.

"A brilliant book ... should be read by everyone interested in the market" The Bull & Bear Magazine, USA

"Among the modern classics in stock market literature. A veritable bible" Miami Herald, USA

Rs. 280/- No. 440-6

Investing Under Fire
Winning Investment Strategies from the Masters for Bulls, Bears, and Bewildered Investors

Alan R. Ackerman, editor

The initial years of the 21st century have thrown up for investors a most complex cycle of uncertainty with the additional risks posed by terrorism and political turbulence added to normal market volatility.

In *Investing Under Fire* a most distinguished assembly of world's leading investment managers review the issues contemporary investors need to consider for investment success. They offer invaluable topical and timeless lessons on controlling risk and selecting profitable investment opportunities:

■ James Awad on small-cap stocks; ■ Vanguard Group founder John Bogle on mutual funds; ■ American Express Financial Advisors' Craig Brimhall on wealth strategies ■ Value Line's Jean Bernhard Buttner on equity research ■ Oakmark Funds' Bill Nyger on the search for value.

"Artfully conceived collection ... combines perceptive commentary on issues of the day with enduring insights on the nature of investing, markets, and human affairs. A valuable resource for investors seeking to understand the forces at play today" Lynn Sharp Paine, Professor, Harvard Business School.

Rs. 395/- No. 567-4

Stock Market Probability
How to Predict Future Events and Improve Your Stock Market Returns using Statistical Techniques

Joseph E. Murphy

This book presents a unique and innovative approach that combines investment analysis the market's probably future. The ability to estimate the various investment outcomes in advance will lead to better-informed decision.

"Brilliant ... refines your decision-making" Business Today

"Clear, concise and informative ... a non-traditional approach to stock market investing" Managing Director, Mitchell Hutchins, USA

Rs. 280/- No. 200-4

TRADING

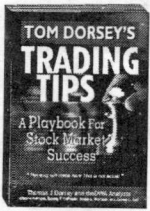

Tom Dorsey's Trading Tips
Thomas J. Dorsey and the DWA Analysts **BEST SELLER**

Tom Dorsey's Trading Tips shows you how to invest confidently using point and figure charting, a proven, objective plan. You will learn: the essentials of stock selection, including a four-step chekclist for starting new positions, how to evaluate technical pros and cons, and how to accurately compare your stocks to market leaders.

"Reading Dorsey's recipe for success is a must" Frank Capiello, President, McCullough, Andres, & Capiello, USA

"A must-read for both the individual investor and the investment advisor" Gino Toretta, Prudential Securities. Inc. USA

Rs. 395/- No. 480-5

Market Neutral Investing
Long/Short Hedging Strategies for Risk Reduction and Return Enhancement
Joseph G. Nicholas

In this book, U.S. investment expert Joseph G. Nicholas explores important new market-neutral approaches to return enhancement and risk reduction.

"A comprehensive road map to market-neutral investing" Gene T. Pretti, Zazove Associates LLC, USA

"A milestone publication, which broadens our knowledge and investment horizons — an invaluable reference tool for portfolio managers ... and the investor community" Sohail Jaffer,

Rs. 395/- No. 538-0

Stock Market Trading Rules
Fifty Golden Strategies
William F. Eng **BEST SELLER**

Stock Market Trading Rules will help you listen to the market. Fifty "Rules," each one a strategic gem, show you how to survive and succeed in the marketplace.

Each of the 50 rules is clearly explained and illustrated with examples of what works, what doesn't and why.

"A great collection of trading rules, and how to apply them to varying market conditions" CompuTrac, Inc., USA

Rs. 225/- No. 343-4

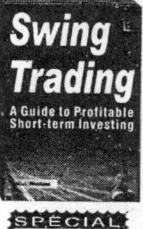

Swing Trading
A Guide to Profitable Short-Term Investing
Marc Rivalland

Swing trading is a method of profiting from the stock market's short-term upswings and downswings. And since such short-term swings are an ever-present phenomenon, knowledgeable swing traders can make money all the time, whether the market is going up or down — or, even, sideways.

Based on the author's two-decade trading experience, this book is packed with expert guidance on a disciplined approach to profitable short-term trading — and one by which you can make money both during the market's upswings and downswings.

"Marc Rivalland offers amazing new insight, clarity and refinement to Gann swing charts" Ashwani Gujral, Author of the bestseller book How to Make Money Trading Derivatives

"You can make far greater profits (by trading) swings than in any other way" W. D. Gann, Legendary Trader

Rs. 495/- No. 666-2

Market Masters
How Successful Traders Think, Trade and Invest & How You can Too!
Jake Bernstein

■ Play your own game. ■ Don't expect immediate results. ■ Do your homework. ■ Don't force trades. ■ Develop discipline, perseverance and willingness to accept losses.

These are just a *few* of the dozens of winning tips you'll find in *Market Masters*. What does it take to succeed? What do winners have in common? How can their experiences help you succeed?

According to Jake Bernstein, great traders are created, not born. Those who lack discipline, persistence and self-confidence lose the never ending challenge of trading profits. But those who survive the battle by using the tools of the masters enjoy the fruits of consistent success.

"Bernstein has done it again! Market Masters ranks among the greatest trading books ever" Commodities Educational Institute, USA

Rs. 395/- No. 411-2

REFERENCE

The Indian Securities Market
A Guide for Foreign and Domestic Investors
Tadashi Endo

BEST SELLER!

An authoritative and comprehensive guide to the operations, regulations and important developments in the Indian capital markets.

This is the first time ever that the practices and regulations of the Indian Securities Market have been documented in an investor-friendly manner.

The author provides a meticulous analysis and description of the Indian capital market based on his experience as an investment banker in both developed and developing countries. The topics covered include: Regulatory and legal framework of the Indian securities market; Trading rules and practices; Custody, settlement and clearing issues, etc.

"The best book on India's securities industry" *Ajay Shah*

"A comprehensive overview... immensely useful"
Business India

"Unravels the complicated operations of the Indian capital market" *India Today*

"Brilliant ... a classic work" *Business Standard*

Rs. 395/- No. 386-8

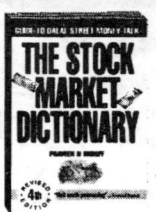

The Stock Market Dictionary
Guide to Dalal Street Money-Talk
Praveen N. Shroff

You probably know about
- bulls and bears ■ cum-bonus and ex-bonus ■ equity capital and reserves.

But do you know what is:
- a white knight
- a teddy bear hug
- the free lunch theorem
- a head and shoulder formation
- cats and dogs

In case you don't, chances are you may not be able to fully exploit investment news or analysis you come across, needlessly losing profitable stock market opportunities in the process.

Here is your guide to all the confusing Dalal Street money-talk you may hear bandied about by "experts". Nearly 2,000 terms are clearly explained by an insider — often with examples and accompanied by hilarious cartoons — to help you make intelligent and profitable stock market decisions.

"Well worth possessing" ... *Financial Express*

Rs. 190/- No. 436-8

EXCLUSIVE CUSTOMER PRIVILEGE OFFER

How to save 15% — rightaway!

On Orders Above Rs. 1,000/- 15% OFF!

At prices substantially lower than charged elsewhere in the world, these professional investment books are great value for money.

Not just that. This Exclusive Customer Privilege offer gives you additional savings:

➤ 15% off on purchases above Rs. 1,000, and
➤ 10% off on purchases between Rs. 395 – Rs. 1,000.

Rush your order using the enclosed Customer Privilege Voucher in this book — or by letter or fax or e-mail to:

How to pay
By demand draft or cheque payable at Delhi/New Delhi, in favour of "Vision Books Pvt. Ltd."

- Please add Rs. 10/- as clearing charges in case of outstation crossed cheques.
- For each book ordered, please add Rs. 10 as postage and packing charges.

Vision Books Pvt. Ltd.
24 Feroze Gandhi Road,
Lajpat Nagar-III, New Delhi-24
Ph: 29836470; Fax: 29836490
email: visionbk@vsnl.com

www.visionbooksindia.com